ACA Books
A Program of the American Council for the Arts
New York, New York

MORE DIALING, MORE DOLLARS

12 STEPS TO SUCCESSFUL TELEMARKETING

Michael E. Blimes ■ Ron Sproat

Book and Jacket Design by Celine Brandes, Photo Plus Art
Edited by Amy Biggers

Director of Publishing: Robert Porter
Assistant Editor: Lisa Glover

Library of Congress Cataloging-in-Publication Data

Blimes, Michael E.
  More dialing, more dollars.

  1. Direct marketing.   2. Telephone selling.
3. Arts—Marketing.   I. Sproat, Ron.   II. Title.
HF5415.126.B58 1985   658.8'5   85-30682
ISBN 0-915400-47-2

This publication was made possible
by the generous support of the
Gannett Foundation

Contents

Preface

Telemarketing is hot. It seems as if everyone is talking about it, a few are even doing it, and still fewer are doing it well. Whether it is for memberships, contributions, or subscriptions, telemarketing has the potential to deliver impressive results. Sound good to you? It sounded good to me, too, 14 years ago when I first participated in what was then called a phonothon. (I know, some are *still* called phonothons.) In some cases, the way these campaigns are conducted has not changed either. They still run as either direct mail *or* telephone campaigns, rather than as a direct-marketing campaign which offers the best of both.

When I hear someone say, "Why should we change, we are satisfied with the results," I think about all the potential that has not been realized. I believe that if they do not change their minds when faced with the facts, then the next change should be in personnel. After all, shouldn't capable managers constantly seek new ways to ensure the financial position of their organizations with even greater earned and contributed income?

In the spring of 1983, I was asked to climb down off my soap box (upon which I stood making grand pronouncements about the potential of direct marketing) and write a book on telemarketing for the American Council for the Arts (ACA). They suggested that I share the body of knowledge I had gained from my successful experience in managing direct-marketing campaigns. I naïvely believed it would not be too difficult and might even be fun. In hindsight, I should have left my phone off the hook. Even the title was hard!

I was grateful for the timely, and capable, writing assistance of Ron Sproat. (After all, a man who has written for the classic television series "Dark Shadows" must have an intuitive understanding of fundraising, membership, and subscription campaigns, as well as the cast of characters usually associated with a not-for-profit organization.) I believe that Ron learned more than he ever cared to know about telemarketing, but to the benefit of the reader who has had limited or no direct-marketing campaign experience.

In truth, if only one organization follows our advice and benefits from this publication, our effort will have been worthwhile. But, please accept this note of caution: *There are no short cuts!* To the extent you try to cut corners — instead of implementing a methodical, marketing approach — you will surely see less than your greatest potential realized.

It is our fondest hope that the information and advice contained herein rings true, and your efforts are all the more successful for the reading.

Michael E. Blimes

CHAPTER ONE

Why the Telephone?

Aside from the broad contact afforded by radio and television advertising, there are three forms of marketing which arts organizations can use to contact prospective donors, members, and subscribers directly: Personal contact, the telephone, and direct mail. A smoothly executed and cost-efficient fundraising, membership, or subscription campaign should use all three of these methods, individually or in combination.

Common sense suggests that face-to-face contact is the most effective, personal form of communication. However, it is practical only in situations where there is sufficient staff to coordinate the many volunteers required to make relatively few contacts. Face-to-face contact can rarely be used as the sole method of solicitation when there are more than 250 prospective donors, members, or season subscribers to contact.

There are some limitations to direct mail as well. Direct mail is frequently very impersonal (Dear Friend...), and communication is one-sided. Mailing costs are escalating rapidly — and you may have to wait months for the responses. One New York City-based arts organization uses highly personalized direct mail for membership and fundraising efforts, and it costs them 70 cents to generate one dollar. That's not very efficient. Very successful mass direct mail programs have been conducted at significantly lower costs, but careful planning and consideration are required.

THE CONCEPT OF TELEMARKETING

No other communication device is as practical, as cost efficient, or as easy to use as the telephone. You can choose not to read mail; you may glance at a solicitation for funds, consider it junk mail and throw it away. But when the telephone rings, it is usually answered. With the telephone, two-way communication is immediate.

Telemarketing is not simply a compromise between the most and least personal techniques. It is an alternative that blends the best elements of personal contact with the efficiencies of direct mail.

The telephone can provide immediate access to a large audience of prospective members, contributors, or subscribers in a relatively short period of time while eliciting the highest probable response. Other forms of mass contact — direct mail, taped messages, etc. — do not elicit an immediate response.

Perhaps the most effective approach, however, incorporates a blend of both direct mail and telephone use. By sending a personalized letter that states your case in advance, the caller can then do a minimal amount of selling over the phone, focusing instead on securing the membership/subscription or on the amount of a donation, with follow-up by mail. This creates a synergism: you get greater efficiency from using both techniques in tandem.

While some consider a telemarketing program to be "cost-effective" when the ratio of dollars spent to returned dollars is equal to 40 percent to 60 percent, recent data suggest that a focused telemarketing effort can produce returns at a ratio of 15 percent to 35 percent, depending on the number and quality of prospects. For example, a well-organized telemarketing effort, implemented, supervised carefully, and controlled, with 10,000 or more good prospects may well generate in excess of $100,000 over three to four weeks at a cost of $15,000-$35,000.

THE PROS AND CONS OF TELEMARKETING

Before launching a telemarketing campaign, it is important to weigh the pros and cons. Here are some ideas you may wish to consider:

PRO	CON
Mass contact with person-to-person dialogue.	People may feel that their privacy is being "invaded."

DISCUSSION: Some people are annoyed by telephone solicitation, and it would be unrealistic to pretend this isn't so. However, a letter of introduction announcing your campaign and your intention to call will help immensely. The caller's use of a carefully written script should offset objections even further. In fact, if your cause is worthy of support, chances are that many people will be glad to hear from you and will be willing to offer their support — particularly if they have supported your cause before.

PRO	CON
Cost-effective performance.	Requires capital investment and equipment, training, personnel, and counsel.

DISCUSSION: This is obviously an extremely important issue, and one that will be discussed at length in subsequent chapters. But generally speaking, a well-run campaign will quickly absorb the initial expenses, and such costs should be included in your budget.

PRO	CON
The response and pledge amount are often immediate.	A phone pledge may not be honored.

DISCUSSION: A number of pledges made over the phone will not be honored. However, that number can be decreased by follow-up mailings and phone calls. If you have planned to accommodate credit cards, payment can be immediate.

PRO	CON
The average gift or membership is higher than that elicited by direct mail.	Cost per inquiry is still cheaper by direct mail.

DISCUSSION: The positive point here invariably outweighs the negative. The simple fact is: more dollars are realized by phone than by direct mail. The excellent cost efficiency of telemarketing has been repeatedly proven in subscription, membership, and fundraising campaigns throughout the country.

PRO	CON
The solicitor can develop a *feeling* about a prospect's attitude, environment, and donation potential through conversation.	The solicitor can't be *certain* of a prospect's attitude, environment, and response. There is no guarantee of a prospect's follow through. You must rely on your telemarketers' instincts.

DISCUSSION: Telemarketing is not a substitute for personal contact. A solicitation visit from a qualified member of your organization is the best way to raise funds, obtain memberships and sell subscriptions. However, personal contact requires a large number of volunteers to contact a limited number of prospects.

PRO	CON
The caller(s) may work from a single site contacting many prospects in a short period of time.	Running a telemarketing site can be taxing. It requires patience, keen marketing insights and proven people-management skills.

DISCUSSION: Organization of a telemarketing campaign can be so frustrating that some groups turn to professional telemarketing organizations. Your alternatives in this regard will be discussed at greater length in the section devoted to the role of counsel.

These are some of the advantages and disadvantages of telemarketing. If your organization decides that these points can all be accommodated, and you recognize the need to contact a broad base of prospective members, donors, or season subscribers, the next step is to determine your potential for success.

CHAPTER TWO

Is Telemarketing for You?

Nothing is more important in telemarketing, or in any kind of marketing for that matter, than the cause. The ultimate success or failure of your campaign depends on the credibility, purpose, and reputation of your organization. If your cause has the potential to attract large numbers of members, subscribers, and/or donors, then your chances of success are increased substantially.

KEY QUESTIONS TO CONSIDER ABOUT TELEMARKETING

The first question to ask yoursef is whether you have access to sufficient funds and whether you are willing to invest them to cover the initial, or all, expenses for equipment, personnel, facilities, counsel, etc.? In some cases, a considerable sum is required initially. Even if you plan to recover the costs, it is still an investment that has an element of risk. The second question is: Are you prepared to justify your actions in case you do not recover your initial expenses? While there is little likelihood of this if your campaign is well planned, you must recognize that the possibility exists. That is why a test phase is always recommended before making a full commitment to a campaign.

If you are uncertain about spending money for a test, the advice of a consultant may be useful in formulating expense and income projections to help in your decision-making process. A consultant can use his or her knowledge of traditional telemarketing responses to make an on-site analysis based on the type of campaign, the cause, the number of prospects, the number of past members, donors, etc.

The condition of your records is a major organizational consideration. If you have kept clear and accurate records of previous campaigns or constituent activity, the projections will be more reliable and a telemarketing program can be relatively simple. Ask yourself these questions:

1. How many potential donors, subscribers, or members are available to you? Of those prospects, for how many do you have fairly reliable information such as name, address *and telephone number?* Are the prospects segmented by categories — past donors, current donors, current members, former members, current subscribers, former subscribers, single ticket buyers, general public, and certain zip code areas or key demographic factors determined from audience surveys?

2. Do you want to contact a closed list (your in-house prospects), acquire new participants from the general public, or both? A closed list will generate the greatest response because the prospects are familiar with your cause and have supported it before. Obtaining prospects from the general public requires patience and is never as cost-effective as a closed list. Even though the telephone offers an effective means to acquire new donors, the cost per contact will be much greater than it will to renew or upgrade past donors, members, or subscribers.

3. How many efficient volunteers are available? Can you afford paid callers? Paid callers are more effective

because they are more accountable, consistent, and available for extended periods of calling.

4. How many of the prospects can be contacted face-to-face in a reasonable period? If you have only one hundred prospective donors, a telephone campaign is unnecessary. If you don't have enough volunteers to contact a large number of prospects personally, then telemarketing and/or direct mail become viable, and necessary, alternatives.

5. How urgent is your need for funds or memberships? The urgency of your need and the probability of success at a reasonable cost-to-generate-a-dollar can often sway hesitant board members to approve the required investment of capital.

If you have carefully considered the previous questions, and have decided that your organization has the necessary information and funds to launch a telemarketing campaign, chances of success are very good. Generally speaking, if you want to contact 1,000 or more prospects for whom you have fairly reliable information, and you have a good cause, you can organize a successful one week telemarketing effort at a reasonable cost.

TESTING THE FEASIBILITY

The best way to determine whether telemarketing is viable for your group is to run a test program. The test should not be a hastily arranged, seat-of-the-pants operation using a few inexperienced volunteers. It should be a scripted and organized effort that follows procedures similar to those described in this book.

A test program requires a significant amount of preparation and initial investment. Some expenses associated with the pilot will be fixed—such as telephone installations and facility preparation. Variable costs include, among other things, payroll for callers, list costs, preparation, and production. A primary difference between a pilot program and a full-scale telemarketing campaign is its size. During the test campaign, at least 1,000 prospects drawn from representative segments of your target audience should be contacted.

For some groups, pilot programs have been so successful that they have led immediately into full-scale campaigns. For instance, one midwestern theatre reported that a three-week test program brought in contributions totalling $61,648 — 54 percent over their goal of $40,000 — plus 1,200 new donors. The test program was such a resounding success that plans were immediately solidified for a five-month extended campaign.

Not every campaign is so successful, however. Many pilot tests fail because the groups in question failed to weigh realistically all the elements involved in a successful telemarketing campaign. The decision to test may be a critical determinant factor; the results should be decisive.

Now, let us consider, step by step, the planning, preparation, and execution of a well-run telemarketing campaign.

THE TWELVE STEPS TO SUCCESSFUL TELEMARKETING

The overall process of running a well-organized and successfully executed telemarketing campaign can be summarized in the following twelve steps:

1. Assess prospective audience potential
2. Establish goals and set objectives
3. Plan the campaign
4. Prepare for the campaign
5. Determine evaluation/control criteria
6. Develop script(s) and probable responses
7. Train staff and callers
8. Test the program
9. Revise scripts and responses
10. Conduct the program
11. Report the results
12. Evaluate the program

During the course of following the first three steps (1. assessing prospective audience potential, 2. establishing goals and setting objectives, and 3. planning), you will gather information with which to make a decision about whether or not suitable potential exists to conduct a telemarketing campaign. You will examine your records to decide on the size and scope of your campaign and to determine the amount of money you hope to generate and the cost of raising it. By the end of Step 3, you should be equipped with a list of good prospects, a campaign objective, a budget, and a timetable. Finally, with all considerations firmly in hand, you will begin the preparations that will culminate in the campaign itself.

The success of your campaign will depend on how well you interpret and follow these telemarketing techniques. Their application must be made with a commitment to simplicity, practicality, and a sensitivity to people.

CHAPTER THREE

STEP 1 Assess Prospective Audience Potential

The first step in determining your audience's potential is to examine the results of your last direct-marketing campaign. Whether it was a campaign using the techniques of direct mail, telephone, or face-to-face solicitation, the prior performance will serve as a benchmark for both previous and potential performance. A careful analysis will also provide a starting point for assessing possible percentages of affirmative response, the number of prospects with an available, current telephone number and home address, average gift, membership or subscription levels, or other criteria you may obtain through a closer look at your records.

Using your past records, divide the total amount of money that was generated by the source of contribution, and segment the audience by dividing past donations into the categories or levels of your program. For instance, your organization may have already estab-

FIGURE 1 ANALYSIS OF THE PREVIOUS CAMPAIGN

DOLLAR RANGE	NUMBER OF PROSPECTS	TOTAL DOLLARS	AVERAGE/ PROSPECT	% OF TOTAL
Under $25	816	$14,930	$ 18.30	14.7
$25-$49	422	15,620	37.01	15.4
$50-$99	225	18,680	83.02	18.4
$100-$249	78	15,320	196.41	15.1
$250-$499	43	16,600	386.05	16.3
$500 and up	25	20,600	824.00	20.2
TOTAL	1609	$101,750	$ 63.24	100.0

lished recognition programs with lists or ranges of donations which qualify supporters such as:

•Donor - under $25

•Associate - $25-$49

•Sponsor - $50-$99

•Patron -$100-$499

•Benefactor - $500-$999

•Inner Circle - $1,000 +

Similarly, subscription records for performance series may yield information about your subscribers such as:

•Balcony subscription

•Mezzanine subscription with and without additional

donation

•Orchestra subscription with and without additional donation

•Box holders with and without additional donations

If such categories do not exist, study your data and establish some categories for segmenting your supporters which will help you with your analysis. One possible breakdown, or audience segmentation, is shown in Figure 1.

To interpret this example, you must recognize the difference between general points of references and specific detail. A general point of reference is that, on average, this organization has approximately 1,600 donors who give an average of $63. However, specific detail reflects more accurately the average gifts contributed by particular portions of the audience.

A direct-marketing strategy might include specific objectives of increasing the average gift given by donors in the first three categories to $22, $42, and $90, respectively, and the number of donors by a conservative 20 percent. This may seem a minor point until you realize that the value of dollars realized would be increasing by nearly $18,000 in the three lowest ranges.

Typical telemarketing campaigns will result in 100 percent, 200 percent, 300 percent or more increases in donors overall. When you consider a similar increase in the higher range, you can better appreciate the excitement generated by telemarketing. This exercise also provides a clearer picture of your core audience—people who have recently supported your organization and are likely to do so again. However, you can add to your list of prospects by looking elsewhere. For instance:

1. **Lapsed constituents.** Look through your records for lapsed members, donors, or subscribers. Often these people can be brought back into the fold with a persuasive phone call, so they should be contacted even if they didn't give or renew during your previous effort.

2. **Lists of those who have indicated an interest in your organization.** Many not-for-profit organizations, such as museums, keep lists of visitors. Performing arts groups often keep lists of people who are interested in upcoming events. If your organization has a similar list, use it to your full advantage. These people have already indicated an interest in you.

3. **Lists of like or allied organizations.** Cultural organizations within a community are often willing to share their lists. If, for example, you represent an opera company, and the symphony orchestra is willing to share its list of subscribers, you may find a potential audience among its supporters.

4. **Prepared lists.** You may want to contact list brokers, who can supply you with lists of likely prospects for a fee. These lists are generally segmented by zip codes, neighborhoods, market areas and other demographic selection criteria. Analyze the characteristics of your current base of supporters for common traits. They may be able to provide you with a potential audience you would

have otherwise missed.

After compiling your list of prospects from all available information, segment the audience further by the relationship to your cause. For instance:

1. Past donors you are trying to get to renew or upgrade their contribution

2. Lapsed donors whom you want to reactivate

3. New prospects from an arts-related or similar interest list

4. New prospects from a demographic list

Divide current contributors by their most recent level of support. Then tally the number of individuals in each of these categories, the amount of money received, and calculate the average gift. While these figures may differ from those in the previous exercise, they are averages based upon specific categories of prospects whereas the earlier averages were based upon general ranges. To the extent that you can plug in the type of prospect and their respective levels of participation in your overall analysis, your projections will be all the more accurate.

For new prospects or lapsed members, figure them in on the lowest possible level (e.g., $1-$25). This information is helpful in predicting levels of support. It will also help you to decide which segments of your audience should be contacted first.

In a telemarketing campaign to contact 10,000 or more prospects, you may expect to make contact with 50-80 percent of the target audience. Callers should secure commitments from approximately 50-60 percent of the contacts who have prior records of support, and 15-45 percent of those with no prior participation. An average return of $25-$45 in broad-based solicitations can be expected. The results should total $125,000-$150,000 at a cost of approximately $40,000. For example:

No. Prospects	No. Cntctd	% Cntctd	No. Dnrs	Avg. Gift	Total Dollars	Cost	Cost Per $
10,000	6,000	60%	3300	$40	$133,000	$40,000	$.30

From this base of information, you are now ready to translate the audience's potential into specific goals and objectives for your campaign.

CHAPTER FOUR

STEP 2 Establish Goals and Set Objectives

In planning your telemarketing campaign, you must (1) establish goals for dollars and donors, (2) examine your resources and capabilities, (3) plan the campaign to realize your potential, and (4) determine your costs. One step follows another, so let's examine them one at a time.

ESTABLISHING GOALS

Establishing your goal is a relatively easy matter. Simply determine your needs and set your goal accordingly. Once you have set the goal, it may be immediately apparent that your needs are too great to be met by telemarketing alone. Remember that you will not reach your total audience by telephone—you can expect to reach approximately 60 percent of your prospects. Contacting the remaining 40 percent may be vital to the success of your campaign. Consequently, telemarketing is one of several options which should be used together—telemarketing efforts are greatly enhanced by face-to-face and direct mail solicitation.

To a certain extent your goal dictates the means you choose to achieve it. For instance, if you need to raise $10,000 and have a list of 2,000-3,000 good prospects, 80 percent of whom have given before, then there is a good chance of meeting your goal with a short-term telemarketing campaign supplemented by an introductory letter for each prospect and follow-up letters for prospects you are unable to reach. On the other hand, if you need to raise $100,000 and have 10,000 prospects, but a large percentage of those prospects have never given before, you will probably need to supplement your telemarketing campaign with other marketing techniques. If you need to raise $500,000 or more, a single telemarketing campaign (or any marketing campaign, for that matter) will probably not suffice—you may need to implement a series of short-term campaigns over a longer period of time to meet your goal.

SETTING YOUR CAMPAIGN OBJECTIVE: DOLLARS OR DONORS?

In planning the campaign, you must decide whether your organization's emphasis will be on dollars or donors. You will acquire more donors if you ask for less money. Conversely, if you key in on a smaller number of select prospects at higher levels of giving, you will obtain fewer donors.

Some groups prefer to place their emphasis on donors. For example, a large metropolitan orchestra recently conducted a campaign to enlarge its subscription lists, with the emphasis on acquiring as many new subscribers as possible. The bulk of the capital they needed was raised from a few large contributors, so the thrust of the campaign was to acquire a new audience that might, in time, make the orchestra self-supporting. In this case, they were willing to compromise the size of the total funds raised to build for the future.

Of course, most groups want both dollars and donors. The two can go hand-in-hand because a campaign to raise dollars usually will result in new donors. For instance, one midwestern theatre acquired 1,200 new donors in their campaign to raise $40,000. A symphony orchestra picked up 1,500 new donors in their campaign to raise $125,000. Whatever your objective, you must decide early in planning your campaign where the emphasis will be—on dollars or donors. If you want both, then in what ratio?

A simple illustration may give you a clearer picture of your situation. Let's say your group requires $100,000 in income generated from contributions. Break down the probability of the following:

One gift of $100,000 equals

One hundred gifts of $1,000,

One thousand gifts of $100, or

Ten thousand gifts of $10

Note that two pyramids form when you stack these up:

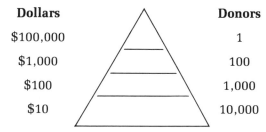

Dollars		Donors
$100,000		1
$1,000		100
$100		1,000
$10		10,000

If the donor goal is most important to you, then you would naturally contact every potential donor on your lists. If the $100,000 objective is more important, then you work backward to determine how many gifts at a reasonable dollar average would be required to equal $100,000. Then figure what percentage of response is necessary to realize that number of donors.

Here is a more concrete example. Let's say you represent a metropolitan museum that needs to raise $100,000, and your list of total prospects (new and old) has been broken down into the following:

Dollar Range	Number of Prospects	Total Potential	Dollar Average
Under $25	4,000	$80,000	$20
$25-$49	3,500	$87,500	$25
$50-$99	2,150	$107,500	$50
$100-$249	275	$27,500	$100
$250-$499	125	$8,750	$250
$500 and up	50	$25,000	$500
Total	10,100	$327,250	

Or in terms of the pyramid:

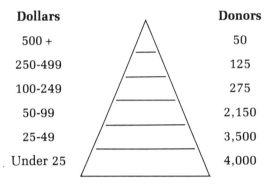

Dollars		Donors
500 +		50
250-499		125
100-249		275
50-99		2,150
25-49		3,500
Under 25		4,000

Add the total potential to be raised if every prospective donor were to give at the level projected. In this case, the total is $327,250. Of course, not all of your prospects will give—the average telemarketing response is 30–50 percent. Therefore, by taking 30 percent (using the lowest percentage) of $327,250, you would set a probable projected dollar goal of $99,083.

In calculating your probable results, you must remember that different segments of the target audience will generate different responses. Any segment not having prior association with your organization will usually generate a low response—the general public may generate a favorable response as low as 8-10 percent. On the other hand, contacting those segments closest to your organization—such as last year's donors—may result in as many as 60-80 percent affirmative responses.

PLANNING YOUR CAMPAIGN: KNOW YOUR PRIORITIES

Meticulous organization is mandatory in any well-run telemarketing campaign. First, as discussed earlier, your list of prospects should be divided into target groups similar to the following:

1.   **Those who have given large amounts previously.** Members/ donors who have given $500 or more should, if possible, receive a personal visit. If a personal visit is impossible, then contact them by phone, but use your best callers. Since you will need time to determine who your best callers are (and even your best callers will need time to

perfect their telephone techniques), postpone calling your top prospects until you are reasonably certain they will be approached in the best possible way. As a word of encouragement, gifts of $1,000, $5,000, and more have been pledged over the telephone; an approach at even the highest levels can work—if appropriate and necessary.

2. **Those who have a consistent record of giving.** These are some of your best prospects, so treat them accordingly.

3. **Those who have indicated an interest in your organization, but have not given recently.**

4. **Those who might have an interest in your organization.**

5. **The general public.** The last three categories would be prospects expected to generate lower levels of response, the general public being the lowest.

Contact these prospects in the early stage of your campaign so that the campaign will build, rather than lose, momentum. Know your prospects as well as your priorities. You will not have much information on *all* the prospects, but plan to gather as much information as you can (e.g., similar-interest causes or organizations they belong to, why they might be interested in your organization, etc.) and impart that information to your callers. The more information you can gather about each prospect, the more your callers will be able to sell your cause in a personal way. People are more likely to give if they are approached as individuals, and are made to feel that their contribution is important to a collective cause.

A WORD ABOUT COSTS

At this point, you should decide on an amount that you will consider as reasonable campaign costs for each dollar you raise. Some telemarketing campaigns have cost as much as 60-70 cents per dollar raised and have been considered successful. Others have escalated to 80-90 cents per dollar raised, and their sponsors were pleased with the results because they showed a profit.

However, if revenue is your primary objective, *an efficient telemarketing campaign should not cost you more than 30 cents per dollar raised.* This is a benchmark figure, a goal you should set now, and keep in mind as you plan your budget.

THE ROLE OF COUNSEL

The role of counsel is an important issue. When should you seek professional help? Professional help can be useful if your organization does not have the experience to organize, implement, and supervise a campaign effectively. Such help is usually in the form of a consultant or an outside agency. In either case, make sure the agency or individual has experience with successfully organizing similar types of campaigns. Simply because someone is in communications, or is a membership or fundraising consultant, does not mean he or she is able to properly execute your organization's telemarketing campaign.

A consultant can evaluate records and help to make difficult decisions. For example, you may be undecided as to how large a gift to request. Naturally, you don't want to ask for too little; on the other hand, you may lose prospects if you ask for too much. A consultant can help you to decide, based on knowledge of similar campaigns. The consultant also can review records and predict probable decreases as well as increases. In general, such an objective assessment will result in more accurate dollar projections than might otherwise be determined.

There are a variety of ways in which counsel may be employed, ranging from no involvement at all to conducting the entire campaign for you. Consider each of these and decide which is best for you.

1. **In-house without a consultant.** Various agencies offer seminars and training programs in telemarketing. These programs can sometimes prepare you to do an adequate job if you decide to take a do-it-yourself approach. However, be warned: organizations have also made costly errors using this approach, and have lost thousands of dollars by not using counsel.

2. **In-house with a consultant.** Another option you might consider is to conduct your own in-house campaign while employing the talents of an outside consultant. The consultant writes the script, trains the personnel, helps to screen and hire callers, trains the initial callers, sets up the calling routine, continues training during the initial calling days, and makes any necessary adjustment in the script and procedures, as well as supervises the pilot program. This leaves you responsible for the subsequent

campaign, but helps you to avoid expensive errors at the outset. Counsel may be recalled if problems should arise or if there should be a decrease in your results and a re-evaluation is necessary.

3. **In-house with a telemarketing firm.** In this situation, the telemarketing firm does everything — it hires, trains and supervises callers, as well as performs such tasks as getting phone numbers and sending out pledge reminders and taking care of the clerical work. The fee will depend on who does what, so you must have a clear idea of the assignment of tasks before you negotiate terms.

4. **A telemarketing firm using its own facilities.** A telemarketing campaign can be grueling; some organizations decide to turn everything over to an outside firm. One major objection to this is the feeling that an outside firm cannot be as knowledgeable about the cause as is the group itself. On the other hand, an outside firm will have trained backup personnel to maintain high-quality performance, and its reputation will ride on your success. Also, the use of an outside firm is often a viable option because it enables you to avoid the high overhead costs of setting up and maintaining an in-house operation.

If you feel you are not experienced or qualified enough to manage a telemarketing campaign by yourself, then the use of counsel in one form or another is highly recommended. While it is not an inexpensive route, the real cost of proceeding without counsel may be more expensive in the long run.

CHAPTER FIVE

STEP 3 Plan the Campaign

The ultimate goal in the planning phase of your telemarketing campaign is to construct a realistic program and budget to present to your board of directors. Your dollar goal and the cost of raising it should provide much of the information you will need for the board to reach a decision. If your organization elects to proceed, you will conclude the planning phase of your campaign by working out a timetable.

ASSESSING WHAT YOU WILL NEED

Before calculating your budget, you must first assess your needs for staff, materials, equipment, and space. Let's discuss these items individually.

STAFF REQUIREMENTS

Your first decision in planning is to decide how many callers you will need. The number of callers depends on the number of phone calls you wish to make. That, in turn, depends upon the size of the target audience and the projected dollar and participation goals.

Based on findings from previous campaigns, an average caller should elicit at least two positive responses per hour. If the overall average gift or commitment projected is $30-$40, an acceptable dollar average per caller per hour is $70. If your membership level, for example, is $25, the average per caller per hour would be $50. If your average subscription is $50, you might generate $100 per hour, per caller, etc. With this knowledge, and for the purposes of this example, the number of caller hours and the number of callers required to meet a goal will be projected based upon the $30-$40 average. Therefore, to figure out the number of callers required for a group which has a goal of $100,000 and an audience of 10,000 prospects:

1. Divide the $100,000 goal by $70 (the amount to be raised per caller, per hour) to get 1,429 hours required.

2. Divide 1,429 caller hours by 40 hours, or the equivalent of one full-time caller week, and get 35.73, or, roughly 36 weeks.

3. Now divide that by a timeline of, say, three weeks, and the result is that 12 callers will be required over a three-week period, working 40 hours per week. Recognizing that this is the equivalent of 12 full-time positions, you will want to recruit more than 12 to accommodate attrition and scheduling complications.

For a group of 12 callers, an administrative assistant and a secretary will be useful if not essential. The administrative assistant may provide operating assistance to counsel, or at least be charged with tabulating results, preparing progress reports, and coordinating logistical details. The secretary types original materials and scripts, as well as retypes revised scripts and responses, daily or weekly reports, and pledge confirmations as needed. The administrative assistant and secretary may be recruited from within your organization or may be hired on a part-time basis from outside. Also, someone familiar with telemarketing campaigns should be available through each step of your planning.

If you do not use counsel who also can and will supervise the effort, you must include a campaign manager or supervisor to manage and motivate the callers. If counsel is not used, such a manager should have extensive, successful experience in similar endeavors.

MATERIALS

The Advance Mailing. A letter is needed for every prospect. The letter should be short and succinct, serving to announce the campaign, substantiate your cause, and encourage your prospects to participate. Plan to enclose a brochure with the letter, but *not* a response envelope. A response envelope makes it too easy for the individual to respond immediately, when there is not a fixed level, by giving the least amount desired. Enclosing an envelope invariably results in a much smaller amount than you would get with a phone call. (In other words, this letter should be an announcement, not a solicitation.) However, there are always exceptions: If you have one membership or subscription level (e.g., $25), you can enclose an envelope — so long as you provide a means to remove the names of those who respond from the list of prospects being contacted.

A personalized letter with first-class postage works best. First-class postage says, "I am important, not junk mail." The signature, whether it is printed or hand-signed should be done in blue ink. If the letters are personalized on a word processor, you will need enough stationery on continuous form computer paper for each prospect. You will also need enough #10 plain or window envelopes printed with your return address only — not necessarily with your organization's name — to do the mailing.

The Telemarketing Form. Each solicitation should be documented on a calling form. You can use anything from a three-by-five inch file card to a multi-part, self-carbon telemarketing form, but the multiple-part telemarketing form is the most cost-efficient when you must use a manual follow-up, reminder process. Since you must decide now whether or not to order them, let's spend a moment discussing the suggested telemarketing form.

A typical form is an 8 1/2" x 11", four- to five-part self-carbon (no carbon paper) form. Computer generated (though it can be run through a typewriter if you do not have a computer), the form includes such information as: (1) name and address of prospect, (2) spouse's name, (3) day phone, (4) evening phone, (5) title and position of the prospect, (6) place of employment, (7) business address, (8) whether or not the employer is a matching gift company, (9) individual donation history (the amounts and dates for one year back, two years back, cumulative, date of last transaction, amount of last gift).

The form should have an "action box" for the caller. This is an area of little boxes indicating dollar amounts (e.g., $25, $50, $75, $100, $250, $500 and "other"). The caller simply checks the box next to the appropriate donation, membership, or subscription. A space should be provided for the prospect who agrees to give, but does not wish to specify an amount on the telephone.

The telemarketing form should provide space to indicate the reason for a refusal — whether a contact is unable to give, unwilling to give, or is not giving because he or she already gave, or subscribed, or recently became a member. If the latter is the case, it is good practice to indicate when payment was made, amount of payment, and to verify it.

The lower portion of the form — roughly one-third to one-fourth of the sheet — is sent by the caller to the prospect to confirm his or her pledge. It thanks the individual on behalf of your organization, and leaves a space for the caller to sign and add a personal thank-you note. The caller fills in the amount and date of the pledge, so the form also serves as a reminder of intent. In addition, the form states that the gift is tax deductible, and that their check should be made payable to your organization.

The form should be perforated so that the lower, billing portions can be detached and fit into both a #10 window envelope and a #9 business reply envelope. The name and address of the prospect should be positioned so that it shows through the window when put into a #10 window envelope for mailing the confirmation of commitment and subsequent reminders.

The second and third copies of this form are different colors. These are your follow-up, reminder notices. They are identical to the first except for an overprint in red that says something like: "Just a reminder in case you have not recently sent your check." If you have not received the pledge payment, membership, or subscription check within three or four weeks, you send out the next copy. If a month later you still do not have the response, the second reminder is sent. A typical telemarketing form is shown in Figure 2.

In summary, the telemarketing form is highly recommended because it serves four important functions: (1) it provides your caller with a past and present history of your prospect's relationship with your organization; (2) it serves as a single working document for contacting the prospect and recording the results; (3) it serves as a follow-up mailing to thank the prospect for the pledge and to remind

FIGURE **2** **THE FIVE-PART TELEMARKETING FORM**

REMARKS:

☐ DECEASED – Remove from file. SOURCE: _____

ne _____
ne Add. _____
_____ ZIP _____
ne _____

.loyer _____
.ress _____
_____ State _____ ZIP _____
._____ Phone _____
:hes Gifts ☐Y ☐N   Ext. _____

.se _____
loyer _____
.ress _____
_____ State _____ ZIP _____
_____ Phone _____
:hes Gifts☐Y ☐N   Ext. _____

.ations with WAC/Member organizations:
_____
_____
_____
_____

CONTACTS ATEMPTED: _____ PERIOD BEGINNING: _____

WEEK	NO ANS.	NOT HOME	LINE BUSY
1			
2			
3			

☐Wrong Number – Reprocess
☐Unpublished
☐Moved
Source: _____

Membership History

	AMT	DATE	M/S	GIFT $
1 YR BACK				
2 YR BACK				
CUMULATIVE				

YES
☐$25 Membership
☐$50 Membership
☐$100 Corp. Memb.
☐ Other: _____

MAYBE
☐Send material; will consider
  ☐Membership; Level: _____
☐Third party said send info

REFUSAL
☐Unable to join now
☐Unwilling to join
☐Already joined
  When: _____ Level: _____

DATE OF CONTACT: _____ **CALLER:** _____

WAC

hington Arts Council
Arts Drive
hington, US 99999

Thank you for your interest in the **Worthington Arts Council**. For more than ten years, WAC has been a vital force in shaping the arts in Worthington. Now we need your support to sustain the active and vital role that the arts play in our community. By joining WAC, you will be adding your voice to the thousands of others who care about the quality of life in Worthington. As a member, you will receive the WORTHINGTON ARTS LINE—our calendar of events—and discounts on tickets to selected performances and exhibitions.

Sincerely,

_____
For the Worthington Arts Council

.SE ENTER MY/OUR NAME FOR:

.nnual Membership which includes a ubscription to the *Worthington Arts Line*. 'nclosed is my check in the amount of:

☐$25 Associate Member
☐$50 Individual Member
☐$100 Individual Patron membership

.recognition of WAC's contribution to the arts in .rthington, I/we enclose a gift in the amount of $ _____.

.e prefer to charge this membership/gift to the .he following account:
☐American Express ☐Visa ☐MasterCard

.int # _____ Exp. _____
.ure _____

CONFIRMATION

Please return this form with your check or charge for payment. Membership reminders are mailed periodically; your prompt payment would be greatly appreciated.

him or her of the amount; and (4) it serves as a second, third or fourth follow-up mailing to prospects who are slow in responding. You will need a form for each prospect you plan to contact, with extras for corrections or substitutes. Above all, using a telemarketing form will save you substantial amounts of time, both for your callers and for your staff. Choosing not to use a form will result in wasting a lot of time doing manual typing, requiring a much larger staff and working in a much less cost-effective campaign environment.

Other Materials. You will also need a #10 window envelope for each prospect who has pledged to give, and extra envelopes for follow-up mailings, #9 postage-paid business reply envelopes, and miscellaneous office supplies (pens, pencils, pads, paper clips, etc.), the amount of which will depend on the size of your campaign.

SPACE REQUIREMENTS

A telemarketing campaign requires a large room for the callers, approximately 400-600 square feet, with separate office space for campaign management and/or support staff. Ideally, callers should be seated together; productivity is heightened in a mutually supportive environment in which callers are able to observe and listen to other callers' techniques. This is a team approach and reinforces the prospect of a successful effort.

EQUIPMENT REQUIREMENTS

A word-processing system, either your own or an outside system, is invaluable in producing the personalized advance cultivation letter, internal reports, and scripts. A touchtone telephone is required for each caller (if the campaign is long-term or will occur for a significant period of time each year, headsets may be a good idea). In addition, a telephone service observing system is a useful device that can monitor the callers without distraction. Too often, not being able to monitor both sides of the conversation has proven to be a source of less than effective evaluation of even the most successful caller's performance.

If return calls are anticipated, you will need a separate, incoming line with a receptionist. You do not want calls returned to specific callers, where chances are that the prospect will continually get a busy signal or a caller's productivity will be disrupted.

CONSTRUCTING A BUDGET

The key to a successful effort may well be the accurate anticipation and allocation of resources to meet expenses. Often, the "penny-wise and pound-foolish" fall short of their goals because they try to skimp on necessary, appropriate expenses (e.g., personalized cultivation letters sent first-class, postage-paid business reply envelopes, touch-tone phones, paid callers, and adequate support staff). They may think they are saving thousands of dollars — but they are doing so at a cost of possibly tens of thousands of dollars. The budget must reflect the costs of staffing and management, counsel, facilities, equipment, postage, printing, and materials.

STAFFING AND MANAGEMENT. For a three-week campaign, approximate staffing costs will be:

Supervisor (other than counsel) . . . .$1,500 to $2,500
Administrative Assistant . . . .$1,000 to $1,500
Secretary $1,000
Callers $8,640
(12 callers a day for eight hours at $6.00 an hour over the fifteen days of the campaign).

The use of paid callers vs. volunteers is often considered to be a debatable issue, but there has rarely been a volunteer-based campaign that can compare favorably to a paid-caller campaign for total productivity. While volunteers may have the best of intentions, they tend to be inconsistent and not truly accountable for their performance. The recommendation here is to use paid callers with payment of at least $6.00 an hour. This may be a higher hourly rate than you think you need to pay, but it will attract a high caliber of callers. If they don't perform, their employment won't continue, and well-paid workers are anxious to keep their jobs and perform well. If callers are efficient, then their productivity is going to more than compensate for the $6.00-an-hour wage. If the campaign is going to continue for more than six weeks, you should consider increasing your pay scale to $7.00 an hour. And for those callers who move into supervisory roles, perhaps even $8-$10 per hour.

Incentives for callers are recommended — in the form of bonuses, premiums, and parties. Bonuses or premiums, though, should be distributed only when the commitments generated are fulfilled to minimize the possibility of "padded" results or too liberal an interpretation of the prospects' intentions.

Commissions are contrary to a team spirit, placing too much emphasis on self-initiative, and too little on group cooperation. In other words, why should a caller share his or her technique with someone else who might be a rival for a commission?

Commissions also restrict your ability to match certain prospects with specific callers. During the course of your campaign, you may find that some callers will be quite adept at raising a $10 pledge to $25, but not so good with the $100 prospects. There will also be callers who handle the $100-and-over prospects quite well. Both are valuable to you, and once a pattern is apparent, you will want to match specific callers with prospects at the level they handle best. In this situation, giving a commission on dollars or individuals pledged or committed can be discouraging and unfair to callers whose forte is soliciting smaller pledges. Consider only bonuses for numbers of pledges made as well as dollar amounts or totals.

COUNSEL Costs for counsel should be incorporated into the budget as well. These costs should include professional fees for counsel, as well as out-of-pocket expenses for transportation, hotel, materials, and report preparation. Such costs will be approximately one-fourth to one-third of your budget if you require full-time, on-site management.

FACILITIES. As noted earlier, you will need a room for calling, the size of which depends upon the kind of logistics you require and physical installations you can obtain. The budget should reflect the kind of costs you will incur to gain access to this type of space.

EQUIPMENT. Telephone installation, equipment, and related charges for 15 to 18 phones will cost from $2,500 to $3,000 for the three-week program that is discussed in this book. If your campaign will include long-distance calling, additional costs must be considered. (You may contract with a discount service or gain access to a corporate service as a contribution.)

MATERIALS. Costs for your telemarketing forms and other materials (e.g., pens, pencils, paper clips, envelopes, postage) must be included as well. If you use the telemarketing forms recommended earlier, they will cost approximately $3,000 to $3,500 for a quantity of 10,000 to 15,000.

ENVELOPES AND PRINTED FORMS. Build in costs for the #10 standard plain window envelopes and for #9 business-reply en-

FIGURE **3** **A SAMPLE TELEMARKETING BUDGET**

Staffing and Management	$12,000
Counsel	8,000
Facilities	1,000
Telephones	3,000
Envelopes/Forms	5,000
Materials/Supplies	1,000
Postage	4,500
Miscellaneous	2,000
TOTAL	$36,500

velopes. A #9 envelope can accommodate even corporate-size checks, and is large enough to hold the portion of the telemarketing form to be returned.

POSTAGE COSTS. If personalized letters are sent, use first-class postage—real stamps, not indicia or postage meters. Hire a mailing house if your staff is too limited. But for a prospect audience of 10,000 to 15,000, plan on a minimum of $3,000-$4,000, even $5,000, in postage. This includes postage for your advance mailing, the initial pledge confirmation, the business reply envelope for pledges, and the follow-up mailings. You must figure how many of each, roughly, you anticipate sending, and then figure what the postage cost will be.

MISCELLANEOUS COSTS. You may have to hire a service to run a directory assistance program on a computer to secure phone numbers for you. Some funds for caller incentives should be available as well. (If your callers have managed to raise, say, the $100,000 mentioned earlier, they deserve a champagne party.) Always include a margin in your budget—$1,000, $2,000—to cover costs you may not have anticipated.

BUDGET FOR MAXIMUM COSTS AND MIMIMUM PRODUCTIVITY

Estimate your budget at the maximum cost, then correlate it with minimum acceptable productivity and calculate the cost to raise each dollar. If it is an acceptable amount, the chances are good that you will be pleased with the outcome. In fact, by going into a program anticipating maximum costs and minimum productivity, you may be

FIGURE **4** **WORK FLOW DIAGRAM FOR PLANNING AND EXECUTING A TELEMARKETING CAMPAIGN**

Action Plan and Strategy Development

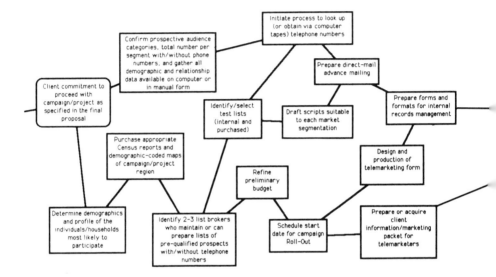

surprised to find your costs are lower, relative to the amount raised, than you originally thought. See Figure 3 for a sample telemarketing budget.

With the budget and the plan for your proposed campaign, you are now ready to meet with the board of directors. If you have used the help of a consultant in planning your campaign and figuring out your budget, by all means ask him to assist you with your presentation. Reluctant boards usually are more willing to listen to an outside expert than they are to a member of their own organization.

BUILDING A TIMETABLE

Assume that the board of directors has given you the approval to proceed. (If they haven't, there is no need to read further.) The final step in planning your campaign is to construct a timetable. Figure 4

Facility Preparation and Telemarketer Recruitment/Training

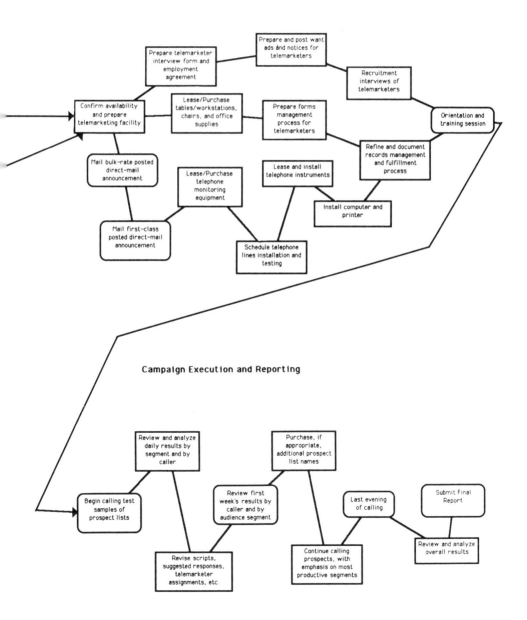

Campaign Execution and Reporting

depicts a model flow diagram for planning and executing a telemarketing campaign. The rounded boxes shown represent milestones around which specific target dates should be set. Milestone dates should be strictly adhered to—missing a milestone date will alter the timing of your entire campaign.

In working through the flow diagram, some of the key elements to be considered in your timetable are:

1. Equipment—telephone and other

2. Preparation of materials

3. Confirmation of arrangement for facilities and preparation of facilities

4. Recruitment of staff and hiring of callers

EQUIPMENT. Telephones, of course, are your primary equipment need. By now, you should have contacted your local phone company to determine costs and scheduling for telephone installation.

Ask your phone representative for a firm installation date; then allow for delays. If your organization is planning to rent or purchase a word processing system, allow time for delivery, installation, and training.

PREPARATION OF MATERIALS. As with equipment, preparation depends upon the budgeted materials. If you have planned to use the telemarketing forms suggested earlier, you must allow time to have them designed and printed. Advance mailings also need to be considered; the letter announcing your campaign will need to be composed, printed and mailed, so allow yourself plenty of time.

If personalized letters are being done on a word processing system, you will need to allow time to have continuous form stationery printed. If you intend to send out a more complicated mailing—such as a brochure or booklet announcing the campaign and giving information about your organization—allow time for writing, designing, printing, and mailing. The advance materials should reach the prospects a minimum of two days or a maximum of two weeks before the phone call, so plan your time accordingly. Also allow time for the acquisition of office materials: sorting boxes for mail, stamps, pads, pencils, paper clips, etc.

FACILITIES. If the campaign is to be conducted in-house, facility preparation must be considered. The preparation of such facilities will be discussed in the next chapter, but allow yourself a minimum of a week to set up properly. If you are renting a facility, consider the maximum length of time you will need it.

STAFF AND CALLERS. If you plan to recruit staff from within your organization, you will still need to know when their services will be at your disposal, so confirm their availability. Delegate responsibilities and plan time accordingly. If you plan to use outside help (such as an administrative assistant and a secretary), leave time to compose an ad and place it in your local papers, to screen calls, and to conduct interviews. The same is true for callers: consider each activity and plan on the time it will take—time for composing and placing your ad, time for screening calls, and the time for conducting interviews.

Calls and interviews alone will probably consume nearly a week, even for a relatively small campaign.

For a three-week telemarketing campaign, a good timetable might be constructed as follows:

1. The first six to eight weeks—prepare materials; confirm arrangements for facilities, telephones, and other needs; assist in the preparation of the advance cultivation packet; hire callers.

2. The next three weeks, conduct the campaign—broken down into the training of callers and testing during the first week, and the running of the campaign during the second and third weeks, with time set aside at the end of each day to calculate specific figures for that day's effort and to rate the performance of each caller.

3. Allot the time necessary to make your final analysis and report.

4. Follow-up mailings four to eight weeks after the campaign.

If your campaign is more extensive than the three-week campaign outlined above, then of course you will need more time to prepare. A sample timetable of an actual campaign is shown in Figure 5.

Overall, the most important thing to remember in constructing your timetable is *to allow yourself plenty of time.* Mistakes happen! Be prepared for them. Be organized.

FIGURE **5** A TELEMARKETING
CAMPAIGN TIMETABLE

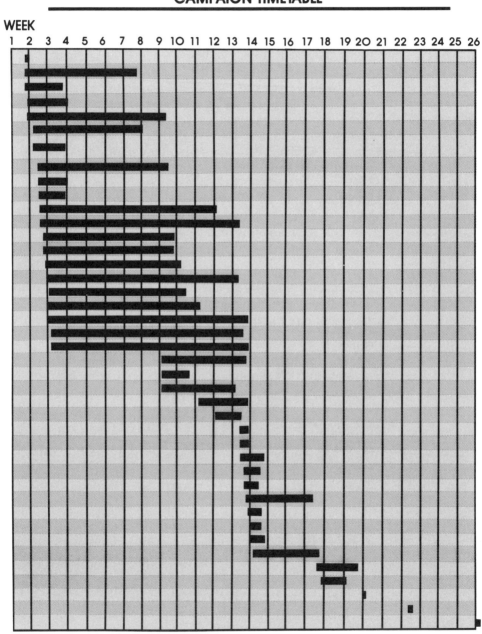

TASK

Commitment to proceed with campaign/project

Determine demographics and profiles of the individuals/households most likely to participate

Confirm target audience categories; total number per segment with/without phone numbers

Prepare and submit action plan

Gather all demographic and relationship data available on computer in manual form

Purchase appropriate census reports and demographic-coded maps of campaign/project region

Identify 2-3 list brokers who maintain or can prepare lists of pre-qualified prospects with/without telephone numbers

Identify/select test lists (internal and purchased)

Refine preliminary budget

Schedule start date for campaign roll-out

Design and production of telemarketing form

Prepare or acquire information/marketing packet for telemarketers

Draft scripts suitable to each market segmentation

Initiate process to look up (or obtain a copy of computer tapes) telephone numbers

Prepare direct mail advance mailing

Prepare forms and formats for internal records management

Confirm availability of a suitable telemarketing facility

Prepare telemarketer interview form and employment agreement

Lease/purchase tables/workstations, chairs, and office supplies

Prepare and post want ads and notices for telemarketers

Prepare forms management process for telemarketers

Schedule telephone lines for installation and testing

Mail bulk-rate posted direct mail announcement

Lease/purchase telephone monitoring equipment

Recruitment interviews of telemarketers

Mail first-class posted direct mail announcement

Lease and install telephone instruments

Install computer and printer

Refine and document records management and fulfillment process

Begin calling test samples of prospect lists

Orientation and training sessions

Review and analyze daily results by segment and by caller

Revise scripts, suggested responses, telemarketer assignments, etc.

Review first week's results by caller and audience segment

Purchase, if appropriate, additional prospect list names

Continue calling prospects with emphasis on most productive segments

Review and analyze overall results

Begin mailing first reminders

Submit final report

Mail second reminders

Mail third reminders

CHAPTER SIX

STEP 4 Prepare for the Campaign

Preparation for your telemarketing campaign will take you from the planning stage right up to the first day of the actual campaign. During this time, you will carry out all the activities outlined in your timetable—and more. You will have to establish your evaluation/control criteria and write your script.

PREPARING MATERIALS AND SECURING EQUIPMENT

Now that you have carefully planned your campaign, step into action:

1. Call the local phone companies and set up the installation of a phone system.

2. Write the letter announcing your campaign, have it printed or prepared for a word processor, and begin production of printed forms, envelopes, and brochures.

3. Gather together the office equipment — typewriters, adding machines, etc.

4. Gather information on donors and prospects. You may be hiring outside services to help you — such as list services, computer services, or services to match existing lists with telephone numbers. Or, if your lists are limited to your local community, you may want to hire a few people — college students, for example — to look up phone numbers.

All these activities will occur simultaneously — so stay calm and keep organized. It is a good idea to call a meeting on the first day of operation. Assemble the people in your organization who will be helping you and discuss everyone's responsibilities.

SETTING UP THE FACILITY

Above all, this large room should be well-lit. Provide adequate space for each caller so he or she has room for the script, the pages of probable responses you will provide, and room to fill out the telemarketing form and/or to jot down information. If possible, set up separate work stations or three-wall enclosures made out of plywood or homosote. Each caller will appreciate the privacy, but will feel a part of the team. The group dynamic is important; if one caller gets a pledge or commitment, the callers on either side of him or her feel they can do the same. If there isn't space for all your callers in one room, put some of them in another room, but keep them in groups.

Set up a standard procedure for processing prospect forms on a same/next day basis. Clearly labeled, standard sorting trays (e.g., with vertical slots) can be helpful. If you include a monitoring system to listen in on calls, the monitoring device should be located away from the callers. If you have provided for return calls on a dedicated line, make certain you have forms for return calls organized at that station and that inbound calls will not disrupt the other callers.

The callers are important to you, so provide for their needs. Find comfortable chairs for them. Set up a rest station for breaks, and keep a pot of coffee on hand. Make certain rest room facilities are adequate. If you are located in the suburbs, make certain parking space is available. Wherever your location, be concerned with regard to security and caller safety (especially at night).

ASSEMBLING STAFF

If you hire an administrative assistant and/or a secretary from outside your organization, try to find someone with prior experience in telemarketing, particularly in the case of the administrative assistant. Volunteers can be useful to you, but *not* as callers. However, they can be invited to observe and learn, and to participate in some way other than telephone contact. Volunteers can look up numbers, help tabulate results, and perform a variety of important, necessary services, such as helping you to set up your calling area.

HIRING CALLERS

The ideal candidate for telephone solicitation is a motivated, confident person with a positive telephone presence — someone who can easily be trained in telemarketing techniques and can follow instructions carefully and cheerfully. Your newspaper ad might read something like this:

Telemarketing. A not-for-profit organization seeks individuals who are motivated and reliable to seek funds.
Pay is $6.00 an hour. The term of the project will last three weeks (give the dates). Training is mandatory and will be provided. Call Ms. Smith at 555-9696.

Candidates should initially be screened over the phone. The telephone interview is as important as a face-to-face interview, so prepare to conduct a fairly lengthy telephone interview. Rate candidates on criteria such as:

1. Voice quality

2. Diction

3. Speed or rate of speech

4. Verbal agility and articulation

5. Attitude

For the first three criteria — voice quality, diction, and rate of speech — ask an open-ended question. For instance, you might ask the candidate why he or she was attracted to your ad. What are his or

FIGURE 6 INTERVIEW EVALUATION CHECKLIST

INTERVIEW EVALUATION CHECKLIST

Name: _____ Date: _____

Telephone No. _____

RATING: Low 1 — High 10

1. Articulate: able to express oneself clearly.

   1   2   3   4   5   6   7   8   9   10

2. Vocabulary: choice of words used to express oneself.

   1   2   3   4   5   6   7   8   9   10

3. Enthusiasm: ability to instill a feeling of excitement.

   1   2   3   4   5   6   7   8   9   10

4. Self confidence: able to convey a feeling of trust in one's powers and abilities.

   1   2   3   4   5   6   7   8   9   10

5. Assertiveness: a feeling of aggressiveness.

   1   2   3   4   5   6   7   8   9   10

6. Analytical: ability of organizing one's thoughts in a clear, logical and persuasive manner.

   1   2   3   4   5   6   7   8   9   10

7. Listening: pays attention when spoken to.

   1   2   3   4   5   6   7   8   9   10

8. Needs employment.

   1   2   3   4   5   6   7   8   9   10

9. Telemarketing/sales experience.

   1   2   3   4   5   6   7   8   9   10

10. Education.

   1   2   3   4   5   6   7   8   9   10

her career plans? To grade verbal agility and articulation, ask questions that require personal opinions and demonstrate the ability to express ideas clearly and cleverly. For example, "What skills do you possess that you feel would make you a good telephone solicitor?" "How important is salary to you?" For attitude, ask questions that relate to stress and the negative aspects of the job. For instance, "What would you do after receiving your tenth 'no' in a row?" "What has been your experience in working for a competitive organization or in a competitive environment?" You will then want to know how long the candidate was employed at his or her last job and what the reason was for leaving. Find out the candidate's work history — are there frequent job changes? (This may not be important to you if you are only hiring candidates for three weeks or short-term projects, but it is important for long-term staff positions.)

Rate the answers on a scale of 1 to 10, one being the lowest and ten being the highest. The best candidates, of course, you will want to see, so schedule an appointment for a 15-30 minute interview.

In the personal interview, tell the candidate something about your organization, then place the bulk of the conversation on him or her. Ask the candidate to tell you something about him or herself, about prior experience, and about interests in the arts. While listening, be prepared to rate the candidate's performance using the checklist shown in Figure 6.

Toward the end of the interview, ask the candidate to read a brief section of a prepared telemarketing script. This is important, as some people do not perform well in person but excel over the phone.

Make no decisions until you have interviewed all the prospects. Advise your most promising candidates that in the event all the positions are filled, there will be a waiting list. Be honest with those in whom you have no interest; tell them no as soon as possible. Be prepared for attrition: people accept jobs, then do not show up on the appointed day, so keep a secondary list handy.

Also, even after you have done your initial hiring, keep notices posted in places where you might find good callers (employment offices of schools and universities, for example, or in the office of your local arts council or your local Actor's Equity), and keep a list of phone numbers, just in case.

So far, we have covered everything in the preparation of your telemarketing campaign except two vitally important steps: (1) establishing evaluation/control criteria and (2) creating the telemarketing script.

CHAPTER SEVEN

STEP 5 Determine Evaluation and Control Criteria

The telemarketing campaign should be monitored daily. This means establishing two sets of criteria — evaluation criteria and control criteria. Evaluation criteria are those criteria by which you can judge your daily performance. Control criteria are the elements you can change to better that performance.

EVALUATION CRITERIA

To evaluate your daily performance, the most basic information you will need to know is (1) the average gift and (2) the number of responses per caller per hour. In addition, the performances of both your audience and your callers may be tracked by recording the following:

- Total hours called;
- Number of calls attempted;
- Number of calls completed;
- Number of affirmatives with a specified amount;
- Number of affirmatives with an unspecified amount;
- Number of affirmatives per hour;
- Percentage of positive responses per call completed;
- Total number of pledges/subscriptions/memberships;
- Total cash dollars committed;
- Average pledge/amount generated

In terms of your callers, also record:

- Average hours per day;
- Average hourly wage;
- Total earned

Finally, to judge how you are doing in relationship to the dollar goal you have set up for yourself, you should tabulate:

- Total expected income;
- Total dollars generated;
- Cost; and
- Ratio of cost to dollars raised

Or, in terms of a donor goal if you have set one:

- Total expected donors;
- Total donors generated;
- Cost; and
- Ratio of costs to donors acquired.

Recording and monitoring all of the above daily, with weekly and monthly summaries will give you an accurate picture of your campaign's success.

CONTROL CRITERIA

If you find that you are not doing as well as you had hoped, better results may be obtained by altering elements of the campaign that you control. These elements are:

- The script

- Your callers

- The time of calls

Even if the troubled spots seem immediately apparent, constant examination of control elements may help to achieve better results.

THE SCRIPT

By altering your script, you may be able to overcome unforeseen audience resistance. For example, you may be trying to convey too much information too soon. If so, you may win over more prospects by eliminating unnecessary talk and getting right to the point. Sometimes, certain benefits will appeal to some segments of your list and not to others. In this case, you will want to change the scripts to emphasize such benefits to the prospects who are most attracted to them, and de-emphasize them or stress other benefits to prospects for whom there is no appeal. Similarly, you may initially emphasize one aspect of your cause and find that prospects respond positively to your organization for an entirely different reason. If so, you should change the emphasis of your scripts to reflect that.

THE CALLERS

The callers should be monitored constantly throughout the campaign, either by a telophone listening device or by simple observation. If you notice a caller who is not communicating, and who is achieving poor results, it is entirely possible (and very likely) that he or she is simply running into a string of poor prospects. You can then work with the caller until you are confident that you have explored every path to improve productivity. Remember, it is probably less productive to start from scratch with a new caller when closer work supervision may turn a caller's performance around.

THE TIME OF CALLS

You won't know until the program test if you have chosen the best time for calling. If many prospects cannot be reached, you may want to change the calling time to later in the day, or from day to night. On the other hand, even though activity during the day may be less than it is at night, it may still be cost effective. If you find that your day callers realize only a small percentage of the amount you raise, you may still conclude that in 15 days of calling, much support will be sacrificed by not using the afternoon time.

Most telemarketing campaigns are in a constant state of flux, particularly during the testing period. Scripts are changed frequently; callers leave, callers are added; approaches are tried, discarded, then tried again with a slightly different emphasis. Setting up evaluation and control criteria at the beginning of the campaign is important because it allows you to see where you are and to make necessary changes quickly.

One more element in the preparation of your telemarketing campaign needs to be considered, and it is perhaps the most important of all: the script.

CHAPTER EIGHT

STEP 6 Develop Scripts and Possible Responses

Like any good play, a well-directed telemarketing program requires a well-written script. Scripts and responses should present your case for support in a succinct and assertive (but not aggressive) manner.

Scripts help to insure uniform control over the solicitations, listing caller presentations and probable audience responses. The scripts will be constantly revised, so callers may make suggestions as they gradually move away from a verbatim presentation, evolving their own individual styles.

THE ELEMENTS OF THE SCRIPT

Scripts should follow a very basic, but effective, outline:

1. Ask for the prospect

2. Identify yourself

3. Establish rapport

4. State your purpose

5. Ask for the amount desired (note incentives)

6. Respond to objections, concerns, excuses

7. Confirm pledge amount, name, and address

8. Thank them and say goodbye

Ask For The Prospect. You must speak with your prospect directly. The most logical approach is to ask for the individual with whom you wish to speak, and if that person isn't home, find out when it would be convenient to call back. Each prospect is an individual who can and should speak on his or her own behalf.

Identify Yourself. Callers should identify themselves immediately. The interaction between the caller and the prospect automatically becomes more personal when each has a sense of the other, even if they are not acquainted.

Establish Rapport. Establishing rapport can be something as simple as: "Good evening, how are you?" Whatever your chosen greeting, you want to reduce the defensive posture that most people assume when they get a phone call from a stranger.

State Your Purpose. When answering a phone call from a stranger, most people wonder why they are being called, so state your case right away. For example, simply say: "I'm calling on behalf of the Worthington Arts Council. I believe you recently received a letter from Bob Smith about our need for your help."

Ask for the Amount Desired (Note Incentives). The first steps in the script are simple and straightforward, but at this point it will need to become more detailed. The request for a subscription, membership or gift must be structured to elicit a positive response. For instance, if you are talking to a past donor, you might say: "Can we count on you for a gift of $100 or would renewal at your most recent gift of $75 be more appropriate?" The question has accomplished three things: (1) The prospect has a choice of two acceptable positive responses—one which is more favorable to you and one which has previously been acceptable to the prospect; (2) You have created a win/win situation, if the prospect agrees; and (3) The caller is showing knowledge of the prospect's past relationship with your cause. If you are offering incentives—a gift or token of your appreciation such as a book, record, poster, or calendar—now is the time to mention it: "By the way, as a means of expressing our appreciation, those who commit at least $500 will receive a signed, limited edition poster from the upcoming arts festival."

Respond to Objections, Concerns, Excuses. Prospects will frequently express objections, concerns, and excuses. These objections will be so varied that probable responses to them all cannot possibly be included in your script. However, in general, the caller should be trained to override objections, concerns, and excuses without sounding hostile or unsympathetic.

Confirm Pledge Amount, Name, and Address. Once a commitment is received for a pledge, a membership, or a subscription, verbally confirm the amount. For example: "Thank you very much for your subscription of $280 for the Spring Classical Series," or, "Thank you very much for your willingness to give $150 to the Worthington Arts Council. Now let me just make sure I have your correct name and address." Then say the name and address, making sure to spell out anything unusual.

Thank Them, and Say Good-bye. Even if prospects have not made commitments, thank them for their time. Although they have said no this year, they may say yes the next time if you are courteous and leave them with a good feeling after the exchange. Courtesy is a long-term investment.

When writing the script, put yourself in your prospect's place. Remember that you are interrupting their afternoon or evening, so be pleasant and polite—and get to the point as quickly as possible. A good script makes a persuasive case in a few well-chosen words. A poor script gives excessive information, taking forever to make the point. There is no surer way to lose your prospect than to bury him or her under an avalanche of words. You may think he or she should know a lot of information but the advance mailing presents an opportunity to tell your story in detail. The call is to close the commitment.

DANGER ZONES

When writing the script, watch out for too many helpful suggestions from well-meaning members of your organization. Do not turn your script over to a committee. Such efforts often result in a long-winded dissertation of the facts about your organization, rather than a simple, cleanly stated solicitation for support. Also, although your callers should personalize the script somewhat, do not encourage embellishment. Insist that the callers stick to the basic points.

Suggested responses to the most likely objections should be prepared and given to the callers for reference. Although your callers should attempt in a positive way to override the objections, concerns, and excuses of the prospects, they should not push too hard. There is a fine line between persuasion and obstinacy, and your callers should know when to stop. For instance, if a prospect cites the poor state of the national economy as a reason why he or she can't give, the caller might suggest that in times like this, the arts need support even more. However, if the prospect says flatly that he or she can't give this year, the caller may make one inquiry about a more affordable donation, but if this is rejected, the caller should quit and thank the prospect for his or her time. Perhaps he or she will participate next year. Your callers should know when and when not to take "no" for an answer. If they don't seem to know, it becomes your responsibility to step in and teach them—and that is not an easy task.

A different script is necessary for each segment of the audience that you are contacting. These scripts may differ only by a word or two ("as a member of our organization, you will realize...," "as a past member of our organization, you will realize..."), or they may be entirely different (as in the case of the general public, where you will want to give more information.) Whatever the case, each script you write should follow the structure of the suggested outline. Sample scripts for different segments of a target audience are shown in Figure 7.

FIGURE **7** **SAMPLE TELEMARKETING SCRIPTS**

SUGGESTED APPROACH TO LAPSED DONORS (UNDER $500)

ASK FOR THE PROSPECT BEING CALLED:	Hello, may I please speak with _____?
INTRODUCE YOURSELF, ESTABLISH RAPPORT, AND EXPLAIN WHY YOU ARE CALLING:	Good evening (afternoon)! My name is _____ and I am calling from Concert Hall on behalf of the Our Town Symphony. You recently received a letter from Jennifer Smith about our need for your help, didn't you?

(If no, or they don't remember: Well, let me briefly sumarize what she hoped to share with you—Friends of the Symphony, such as yourself, have long recognized the need for private contributions to aid the Symphony in the efforts to ensure quality in performance and meet operating expenses. . . .) |
| SINCE THE PROSPECT IS A LAPSED DONOR: $ 35 – SUPPORTERS $ 75 – AFFILIATES $125 – ASSOCIATES $250 – FELLOWS $500 – DONORS | I know that you have helped the Symphony in the past and, as Mrs. Smith noted, we hope you can renew your participation. Can we count on you for a gift of (*next highest recognition level*) so we can add your name to the roster of _____ with all the privileges of that recognition group, or would renewal at your last gift level of $_____ be more appropriate?

(WAIT FOR THE PROSPECT'S RESPONSE) |
| IF THE PROSPECT BALKS AT GIVING THE LARGER AMOUNT: | I can appreciate that the higher level of support may not be practical at this time. Would an increase somewhere between your last gift and the next level be agreeable to you?

(WAIT FOR THE PROSPECT'S RESPONSE)

We would be grateful for whatever assistance you provide. What amount can we count on? |
| WHEN THE PROSPECT PREFERS NOT TO SPECIFY AN AMOUNT: | I understand; you need not feel obligated to specify the amount of your gift at this time. I can send you a confirmation of your willingness to give, along with a postage-paid reply envelope for your convenience, and you can give what you can—would that be agreeable with you? |

IF THE PROSPECT SAYS "NO":	Is there a particular reason you feel you cannot help us at this time?
	(REFER TO THE MOST APPROPRIATE RESPONSE TO OBJECTIONS, CONCERNS, AND EXCUSES)
IF THERE IS NO REASON GIVEN AND THE RESPONSE IS STILL "NO":	Well, thank you for your time and for considering the prospect of making a gift to the Symphony. I hope that we might enjoy your participation as a donor sometime in the future. Good-bye!
IF "YES":	Thank you, (*prospect's name*); I will confirm your willingness to contribute $_____. I am certain that Mrs. Smith and the other Friends of the Symphony will be pleased to learn of your participation.
VERIFY THE ADDRESS: (CHECK SPELLING OF THE NAME, IF UNUSUAL)	We are grateful for your assistance. Now let me just verify that I have the right address for the records: (Check address, city, state, and zip); Is that where you prefer pledge reminders to be sent? Fine! I will be sending a confirmation of our conversation; we would appreciate your honoring your pledge at your earliest convenience. It has been nice talking with you. Thanks again! Good-bye!

SUGGESTED APPROACH TO NON-DONATING SUBSCRIBERS

ASK FOR THE PROSPECT BEING CALLED:

Hello, may I please speak with _____?

INTRODUCE YOURSELF, ESTABLISH RAPPORT, AND EXPLAIN WHY YOU ARE CALLING:

Good evening (afternoon)! My name is _____ and I am calling from Concert Hall on behalf of the Our Town Symphony. You recently received a letter from Jennifer Smith about our need for your help, didn't you?

(If no, or they don't remember: Well, let me briefly sumarize what she hoped to share with you—Friends of the Symphony, such as yourself, have long recognized the need for private contributions to complement subscription income to provide funds to ensure continued quality in performance and meet annual operating expenses. . . .)

SINCE THE PROSPECT IS A SEASON SUBSCRIBER:
$ 35 — SUPPORTERS
$ 75 — AFFILIATES
$125 — ASSOCIATES
$250 — FELLOWS
$500 — DONORS

As a subscriber, you have enjoyed the opportunity to experience first hand the quality in performance we strive to maintain. But, subscriptions alone do not cover all of the operating costs. As a part of the effort to meet those expenses and, at the same time, keep the price of subscriptions as low as possible, we must seek private contributions. Can we count on you for a gift of $35, $75, $125 or more so we can add your name to the appropriate donor recognition roster of individuals who have provided tangible evidence of their support of the Symphony?

(WAIT FOR THE PROSPECT'S RESPONSE)

IF THE PROSPECT BALKS AT GIVING THE LARGER AMOUNT:

I can appreciate that the higher level of support may not be practical at this time—what with the costs of subscription renewal—but we would be grateful for whatever assistance you could provide. What amount can we count on?

WHEN THE PROSPECT PREFERS NOT TO SPECIFY AN AMOUNT:

I understand; you need not feel obligated to specify the amount of your gift at this time. I can send you a confirmation of your willingness to give, along with a postage-paid reply envelope for your convenience, and you can give what you can—would that be agreeable with you?

IF THE PROSPECT SAYS "NO":	Is there a particular reason you feel you cannot help us at this time?
	(REFER TO THE MOST APPROPRIATE RESPONSE TO OBJECTIONS, CONCERNS, AND EXCUSES)
IF THERE IS NO REASON GIVEN AND THE RESPONSE IS STILL "NO":	Well, thank you for your time and for considering the prospect of making a gift to the Symphony. I hope that we might enjoy your participation as a donor sometime in the future. Good-bye!
IF "YES":	Thank you, (*prospect's name*); I will confirm your willingness to contribute $_____. I am certain that Mrs. Smith and the other Friends of the Symphony will be pleased to learn of your participation.
VERIFY THE ADDRESS: (CHECK SPELLING OF THE NAME, IF UNUSUAL)	We are grateful for your assistance. Now let me just verify that I have the right address for the records: (Check address, city, state, and zip); Is that where you prefer pledge reminders to be sent? Fine! I will be sending a confirmation of our conversation; we would appreciate your honoring your pledge at your earliest convenience. It has been nice talking with you. Thanks again! Good-bye!

SUGGESTED APPROACH TO SINGLE-TICKET PURCHASERS

ASK FOR THE
PROSPECT BEING
CALLED:

Hello, may I please speak with
_____?

INTRODUCE YOURSELF,
ESTABLISH RAPPORT,
AND EXPLAIN WHY
YOU ARE CALLING:

Good evening (afternoon)! My name is
_____ and I am calling from Concert
Hall on behalf of the Our Town Symphony.
You recently received a letter from Jennifer
Smith about our need for your help, didn't
you?

(If no, or they don't remember: Well, let me
briefly sumarize what she hoped to share with
you — Friends of the Symphony have long
recognized the need for public and private
contributions to complement single-ticket
sales and season subscription earned income
to provide funds to ensure continued quality
in performance and meet annual operating
expenses. . . .)

SINCE THE PROSPECT
IS A SINGLE-TICKET
PURCHASER:
$ 35 — SUPPORTERS
$ 75 — AFFILIATES
$125 — ASSOCIATES
$250 — FELLOWS
$500 — DONORS

Since you have attended the Symphony, you
have experienced first hand the quality in
performance we strive to maintain. But,
earned income alone does not cover all of the
operating costs. As a part of the effort to meet
those expenses and, at the same time, keep
the price of tickets as low as possible, we
must seek private contributions. We would
welcome the opportunity to add your name to
the distinguished roster of individuals who
have provided tangible proof of their support
of the Symphony. Can we count on you for a
gift of $35, $75, $125 or more?

(WAIT FOR THE PROSPECT'S RESPONSE)

IF THE PROSPECT
BALKS AT GIVING THE
LARGER AMOUNT:

I can appreciate that the higher levels of
support may not be practical at this
time — what really counts is your
participation — but we would be grateful for
whatever assistance you could provide. What
amount can we count on?

WHEN THE PROSPECT
PREFERS NOT TO
SPECIFY AN AMOUNT:

I understand; you need not feel obligated to
specify the amount of your gift at this time. I
can send you a confirmation of your
willingness to give, along with a postage-paid

reply envelope for your convenience, and you can give what you can—would that be agreeable with you?

IF THE PROSPECT SAYS "NO":

Is there a particular reason you feel you cannot help us at this time?

(REFER TO THE MOST APPROPRIATE RESPONSE TO OBJECTIONS, CONCERNS, AND EXCUSES)

IF THERE IS NO REASON GIVEN AND THE RESPONSE IS STILL "NO":

Well, thank you for your time and for considering the prospect of making a gift to the Symphony. I hope that we might enjoy your participation as a donor sometime in the future. Good-bye!

IF "YES":

Thank you, (prospect's name); I will confirm your willingness to contribute $_____.
I am certain that Mrs. Smith and the other Friends of the Symphony will be pleased to learn of your participation.

VERIFY THE ADDRESS: (CHECK SPELLING OF THE NAME, IF UNUSUAL)

We are grateful for your assistance. Now let me just verify that I have the right address for the records: (Check address, city, state, and zip); Is that where you prefer pledge reminders to be sent? Fine! I will be sending a confirmation of our conversation; we would appreciate your honoring your pledge at your earliest convenience. It has been nice talking with you. Thanks again! Good-bye!

CHAPTER NINE

STEP 7 Train Staff and Callers

On the first day of the telemarketing campaign, gather callers and staff together. Your staff, of course, is your administrative assistant, a secretary, and volunteers. Everyone should meet the callers to establish a sense of teamwork.

UNDERSTANDING THE CAUSE

The first hour of the meeting should be spent describing your organization — its history, its purpose, and its goals. Distribute any information you may have about your organization and encourage everyone to study and absorb it. Your callers may need to have this information at their fingertips when they begin to make phone calls. Try to infuse or arouse in everyone — staff and callers alike — enthusiasm for your organization, so do all you can to make them feel at home. In fact, give them memberships, if such exist. If yours is a performing group, arrange for your callers and staff to attend rehearsals and/or performances. If you represent a museum, take them on a guided tour and point out the paintings or exhibits of which you are particularly proud. If yours is an umbrella group for various cultural organizations, let your people experience as many events as you can arrange. The point is to make them knowledgeable about your organization and encourage their interest and enthusiasm for your cause. That enthusiasm will show when they contact your audience.

ESTABLISHING OFFICE PROCEDURES

Next, establish and explain office procedures as they will be followed throughout the campaign. Creating a routine for both the callers and the staff is important to insure a professional, organized atmosphere.

Callers should not be assigned office duties — apart from separating their pledge forms in the appropriate boxes. The reason for this is cost; you will run a more cost-effective campaign if your callers make as many phone calls as possible in the allotted time. Basic office work should be done by your staff. Even so, your callers should understand office procedures so they will know what's going on and be able to fill in if necessary.

Set up a checklist of daily procedures for your staff. These include:

1. Prepare outgoing envelopes — insert business reply envelopes, appropriate information brochures/flyers.

2. Each day, place completed pledge reminder forms in prepared envelopes for mailing and take them to the post office at the end of the day.

3. Sort completed pledge forms by category (e.g., Past Donors, Non-Donors).

4. Within each category, sort as to new or renewed support.

5. Separate and total the number of donors and dollar totals/averages for new, increased, decreased, and the same membership/gift/subscription support.

6. Tally the number of prospects contacted, by categories,

resulting in other responses (e.g., "No," "Wrong Number," "Already Joined/Gave/Subscribed").

7. Summarize the results on prepared report formats and calculate average dollar amounts per prospect and percentages of response by category, type, etc.

LEARNING AND REHEARSING THE SCRIPTS

Next, hand out your scripts and probable responses. Becoming acquainted and comfortable with the script(s) and responses is essential, as your callers must deliver the script spontaneously. Let them read the script aloud. They may want to change a word or two, and perhaps you will, too. However, at this stage of the game, you must insist that they follow the script carefully. Major changes, if any, will come later.

Create some test situations. Have your callers read to each other and listen to each other, one being the caller and one being the prospect. Role playing is a good way to get a feeling for a prospective donor's viewpoint. Continue this process until your callers seem to be comfortable with their scripts. Have your staff join in as well—they may be required to fill in for callers in an emergency.

TEACHING GOOD PHONE TECHNIQUE

Training should include the principles and techniques of telephone usage and etiquette. The basics of good telephone technique, as defined by the Bell System, include the following advice:

1. **Prepare mentally.** Your callers must turn off their own concerns and concentrate on their prospects' needs. They should be enthusiastic and positive.

2. **Prepare physically.** Scripts and probable responses should be readily accessible. Other information you have given your callers about your organization should be at their fingertips (or posted in front of them) so they are never lost for an answer.

3. **Put yourself in the other person's situation.** Your callers

should constantly remind themselves that the purpose of the call is to provide helpful information that the prospect will be glad to hear.

4. **Keep smiling.** "Dial with a smile," and the person at the other end will "hear it."

5. **Be careful of the pitch of your voice.** The other person can't see the caller, so pitch or voice becomes even more important. The pitch should not be too high or shrill; neither should it be too low or gruff. The voice that represents your organization should be friendly, natural, and conversational — and full of confidence.

6. **Use a reasonable rate of speech.** No one likes to be attacked by a fast-talking salesperson. Too slow a delivery invites impatience and interruption. The ideal rate of speech for telephone solicitation is between 120 and 150 words per minute. This also depends on the nature of your offer.

7. **Be a good listener.** When two people are talking, no one is listening. Good callers should also be good listeners. They let the prospect ask questions. They know or learn quickly how to pick up telltale signs of a prospect's concerns, or that he or she is ready to make a decision.

8. **Don't be in a hurry to hang up.** Restate what has been agreed to so there can be no misunderstanding. Thank the person you're calling by name before hanging up. Don't hang up until your prospect does.

WHEN TO BEGIN CALLING

The recommended training period is usually three to four hours on the first day, with the last four hours of that day spent actually making calls. Naturally, you will not give your best prospects to the callers in these situations. Rather, give them a middle-range prospect list. If you find you don't have time for calls, as often happens, at least you have set the groundwork for the next day, which will begin the most crucial part of your campaign: the test.

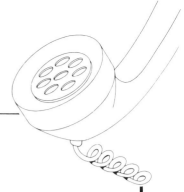

CHAPTER TEN

STEP 8 Test the Program

A telemarketing campaign is always a risk. However, many techniques exist for sampling an audience to determine the *probable* degree of its participation. This is vital to a telemarketing campaign. In fact, the key to a successful campaign might be summed up in three words: test, test, test!

By testing, you will accomplish the following: (1) you can determine staffing needs and time requirements to cover the entire target audience; (2) you can get a sense of the prospect's reaction to the script(s) and responses; (3) you can judge the effectiveness of individual callers; (4) you can estimate percentages of the target audience, by category, that can be contacted and that will participate; (5) you can gauge the average donation, membership, or subscription you will receive, by category; and (6) you can predict the overall productivity of your program. Testing allows a margin for error and provides an opportunity to fine-tune the entire telemarketing process, to revise scripts and responses, and to retrain or replace callers.

HOW TO TEST

Testing means contacting a representative portion of your audience and trying out your script(s). This, in turn, means selecting, at random, an audience of at least 1,000-2,000 members, donors, or subscribers, or roughly 10 percent of your list. Be sure that the test audience proportionately represents each segment of your total target audience. In computing the test results, count only those you have actually contacted and from whom you have received a definite response.

The first week of your telemarketing campaign should be devoted to the test. Using up to 15 callers, you can usually cover 2,500-5,000 prospects in this time. The names should be distributed equally to your callers, all using the same script(s).

Expect this to be a hectic time. Remember that your callers will be working with a new script and developing their own styles of telephone commmunication. It may take them time to find the style that works best, particularly if this is their first telemarketing campaign. Some telemarketing experts recommend that the first 100 calls should not be included in the test results.

Monitoring calls is the best way to know what is happening. If you don't have a monitoring device, stay in the room with your callers during calling hours to listen and assist, or make sure a qualified representative of your organization is there to answer questions and encourage the callers. Make certain the callers are conveying the message clearly. As the person in charge, your presence should be felt without being intrusive. Callers should feel you are there to guide them in case they run into trouble.

JUDGING CALLER PERFORMANCE

In judging the performance of the callers, there are two main ideas for the supervisor to remember. First, the job of caller is not easy. Sounding confident and enthusiastic after half a dozen rejections in a row is difficult. Secondly, it takes some people longer than others to feel comfortable and confident in their role as telephone communicator. Those who continue to feel uncomfortable will probably leave voluntarily after a few days. Those who still show promise but need improvement may be helped either by you, or by other callers who have developed effective techniques they can share. If you have done a good job of screening your callers, they should have shown some aptitude for the job.

However, suppose you were wrong. Suppose you have hired a caller who, for one reason or another, doesn't seem to make the grade. What should you do about it?

Dismiss the caller. In general, there are three good reasons for dismissing a caller: (1) continued poor performance with little likelihood of improvement; (2) reporting inaccurate results (i.e., someone who deliberately counts a "maybe" as a "yes" in recording pledges, thereby throwing off your estimates); and (3) refusal to cooperate (by being lazy, argumentative, and/or, in general, destructive to the team effort).

However, be cautious of dismissing a caller because he or she isn't getting the results you expected. The caller who isn't measuring up to your standards, in terms of getting two affirmative responses per hour, isn't necessarily doing a poor job. He or she may simply be running into a string of poor prospects. This is a primary reason why monitoring phone calls is so important—you need to hear both ends of the conversation to adequately judge performance. Also remember that dismissing a caller for the wrong reason (and dismissing someone for not meeting a quota is the wrong reason if it isn't the caller's fault) can have an adverse affect on other callers.

One recent telemarketing campaign was not the success it should have been, partially because of poor judgment in this area on the part of the organization's staff member who served as the supervisor. The callers were well aware of the supervisor's lack of willingness to work with callers to improve productivity. Their morale plummeted when a caller who had been very productive for several weeks was dismissed after several days of lackluster performance on a particularly difficult portion of the proposed list—nondonors in an average income area. Compassion and a commitment to work with callers are essential.

You will soon find that some callers do better with certain prospects than with others. For example, a caller may be very good in dealing with past prospects, but not so good when dealing with new prospects. You can profit from these discoveries later by matching the right callers with the right prospects.

USING TEST RESULTS

A good goal of the first week is to have gone through a list of 2,500-5,000 prospects with 15 callers. Each evening after calling hours, tabulate and itemize your daily results. This will give you actual results (total dollars generated, cost, ratio of cost to dollars raised) that can be used to define more clearly probable results (based on your 10 percent audience sampling). Armed with this information, you are ready to report to your board of directors. If all has gone well, you will have good news for them. However, even if the results of the test run have been disappointing, it is unlikely that the board will recommend that you shut down your operation at this time. Most of your expenses are incurred during preparation and planning, so you will very likely continue if you show a reasonable net return.

Whatever your results, this is the time to examine the control elements of your campaign (the callers, the script and responses, the time of calling) and to decide how to improve them to achieve maximum results. In particular, your attention should be concentrated on the primary control element: your script.

CHAPTER ELEVEN

STEP 9 Revise Scripts and Responses

Never begin your telephone solicitations until an effective script has been written. You can add or delete information later, based upon the script's performance, but it is important to have a solid foundation from which to work. Major script revisions should be made during the first week—the week of testing—based on the results and the reactions of your prospects.

During the first week, callers and supervisors may suggest alterations in the scripts. Test such proposed changes on a limited basis and, if they seem to be effective, incorporate them into the script(s) and distribute them to the other callers. But, no matter how many times a script may be modified, a caller should be allowed to use the scripts and responses with which he or she can *realize the best results*. There is no reason why two versions of the same script cannot be used simultaneously.

The script is only the base pattern for a dialogue and is not intended to sound as though it is being read. Callers need to know the script well enough to deliver it in a conversational tone. Nothing will turn off a prospect faster than the artificial sound of someone obviously reading from a prepared script.

Callers should be encouraged to develop a flexible, conversational style; not every sentence in the script will be needed. For instance, the advance mailing may have been so persuasive that some prospects have already decided to give. In this case, the caller should skip past the reasons for giving and concentrate on securing the pledge. In other cases, the caller may quickly realize that the prospect knows little or nothing about your organization, and should be prepared to add information. He or she might read from brochures or other relevant material, filling in facts about your organization that may sway the prospect but are missing from the prepared script.

The script should be refined on the basis of audience reaction, the individual styles of the callers, and the interaction between the audience and the callers. In one recent campaign, one caller found his own unorthodox way of obtaining results. He simply announced to the prospect that he was going to ask for $10,000. He waited for the stunned silence then laughed, said he was joking, and went on with the prepared script, asking, of course, for a much lower amount. He also invariably got it. This strategy probably wouldn't work for everyone, and certainly isn't recommended—such an approach requires a very special kind of telemarketer. The point is that the caller absorbed the prepared script, then found his own effective (albeit unorthodox) way of winning over his audience. It worked for him.

Callers should be advised that they are welcome to test their own approaches as long as the basic elements of information are included and *the results are better than those obtained with the prepared script.* Otherwise, the original script should be retained.

By the end of the testing week, you should have a working script, and your callers should have acquired a certain polish in their deliveries. You are now ready to begin your campaign in earnest.

CHAPTER TWELVE

STEP 10 Conduct the Program

In many respects, the campaign is an extension of your test. Your objective now is to take what you learned from the test and use it to construct the most effective campaign possible.

CONSTRUCTING THE CAMPAIGN

In the test, you sampled each segment of your target audience. Members of your audience were chosen randomly to make up your sampling, and the object was to discover how each segment of the audience would respond to your script. In the actual campaign, you want to match the best prospects with the best callers, working from a proven script that states your case in the most effective way possible.

This means choosing your best callers and giving them time to improve. It also means getting your script in the best possible shape. Wait until your operation is running smoothly—until you have experienced, productive callers working from a proven script—before approaching your next prospects. In fact, don't contact the prospects you would consider your best in the first week of calls—not until your script and callers are as polished as they can be. (Your best prospects, of course, are those closest to your organization, such as past members, donors, or subscribers who can be counted upon to give generously.) As you begin to call your better prospects, the results should reach a plateau on your second and third weeks, only to drop off when the list of best prospects begins to dwindle. A typical pattern of response for a telemarketing campaign is shown in Figure 8.

Conducting a telemarketing program is an exercise in human dynamics—the interaction between callers and prospects, as well as among callers and program supervisors and support staff. The person in charge of the program will be responsible for creating and maintaining the best possible working environment. Responsibilities will include: (1) establishing a productive daily routine; (2) creating caller incentives; (3) maintaining caller schedules (including hiring and training new callers); (4) monitoring calls and callers; (5) instilling and maintaining a sense of commitment and momentum; and (6) reporting results. In addition, the entire staff is responsible for (7) sending out telemarketing forms and return envelopes, and (8) tabulating returns. Let's examine each of these elements.

ESTABLISHING A DAILY ROUTINE

To run your campaign as easily and smoothly as possible, first set up a schedule for the supervisor and the staff. Such a schedule might involve the supervisor arriving at least an hour ahead of the callers to make sure the calling area is ready for the day. Caller boxes should be emptied daily. (These boxes, mentioned earlier, should be placed at each caller's station, and labelled for category results, such as various pledge amounts, maybe—will consider, no—unwilling, no—unable, etc.) Caller forms should be sorted and ready. The forms or cards are usually organized in batches of 50 or 100; a caller can usually get through 100 in a four-hour period. Place the batches in an established place so callers can pick them up as they arrive and begin to make calls immediately. The supervisor should schedule time for a short meeting with the staff before callers arrive to discuss special problems, time for photocopying script changes, time for small duties such as making coffee, checking rest rooms, etc.

FIGURE 8 TYPICAL PATTERN OF RESPONSE TO A TELEMARKETING CAMPAIGN

Daily Performance in Securing Commitments

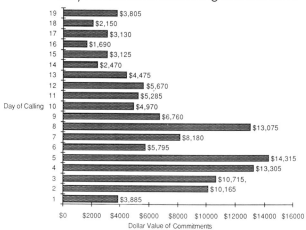

Day of Calling	Dollar Value of Commitments
19	$3,805
18	$2,150
17	$3,130
16	$1,690
15	$3,125
14	$2,470
13	$4,475
12	$5,670
11	$5,285
10	$4,970
9	$6,760
8	$13,075
7	$8,180
6	$5,795
5	$14,315
4	$13,305
3	$10,715,
2	$10,165
1	$3,885

Telemarketing Productivity

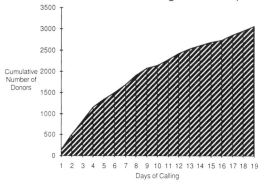

Cumulative Number of Donors vs. Days of Calling

Cumulative Dollar Value

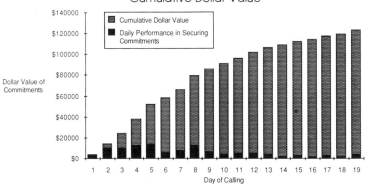

Legend:
- Cumulative Dollar Value
- Daily Performance in Securing Commitments

Dollar Value of Commitments vs. Day of Calling

Staggered rest periods may be scheduled for your callers and staff to ensure a continuous operation. Suppose you have decided on a seven-hour calling day, broken up into two shifts: 3:00 p.m.-6:00 p.m. and 6:30 p.m.-10:30 p.m. The supervisor's schedule might be arranged like this:

2:00-3:00 p.m.: Arrive. Arrange calling room. Photocopy script changes. Brief meeting with staff.

3:00 p.m.: Callers arrive. Pass out script changes. Arrange for changes in caller schedule. See that the calling day begins promptly.

3:00-6:00 p.m.: Monitor calls. Take incoming calls for replacement callers. Be in the calling room at regular intervals to answer questions and attend to caller problems. Tabulate incoming commitment dollars. Meet with members of your organization about campaign results so far.

6:00-6:30 p.m.: Prepare for second shift of callers.

6:30-10:30 p.m.: Repeat activities of earlier shift.

10:30-11:30 p.m.: Callers leave. Do nightly records. Mail forms and return envelopes.

Other duties might include training replacement callers and meeting with callers to discuss changes in campaign strategy. Supervising a telemarketing campaign is an extremely demanding job and is usually too much for one person to do alone. *So be prepared at the outset to delegate responsibility.* Before your campaign begins, assign specific duties to responsible members of your staff.

CREATING CALLER INCENTIVES

While paying commissions is not recommended, you might provide other incentives to your callers. Financial incentives, such as small bonuses, were discussed earlier. Planning a champagne party when you have reached a certain goal is also a good idea. In a large campaign, a series of after-hours parties helps to celebrate achievements along the way. You may use a graph of results in your calling room, showing where you hope to be. Each day, draw a line for dollars and a line for donors, showing your callers how close the "team" is to achieving the goal. In addition to group incentives, do all you can to stress the importance of each caller's contribution in reaching your goal. This means letting each caller know when he or she is doing well. A simple expression of appreciation can be a powerful incentive to do well or to do better. Individual, private reviews should be scheduled as well.

MAINTAINING CALLER SCHEDULES–HIRING AND TRAINING NEW CALLERS

Some callers will probably work part-time and some callers will work full-time on a prearranged schedule. The caller schedule requires flexibility to accommodate sick days or other reasonable excuses.

In the initial stage of your campaign, determine which part-time callers are willing to work an occasional full day. Also, a responsible member of your staff (or two or three) should be prepared to fill in, in an emergency.

Caller turnover is unavoidable, even in a three-week campaign. Most callers burn out after two weeks of making phone calls, so new callers will need to be hired and trained while the campaign is in progress. In the section devoted to hiring callers, it was suggested that you keep a list of alternates after your hiring. These are the people you can now contact.

New callers will learn faster if placed in the same room with experienced callers. However, new callers must be given the same treatment that was given the original callers. You must take the time to inspire strong enthusiasm for your cause.

In a large campaign scheduled to run for months, a pool of callers may be created. This is particularly advisable if your organization is located in a large city where students, artists, musicians and/or actors who are looking for part-time work may be found. These people often make excellent callers.

MONITORING THE CALLS AND CALLERS

Monitoring calls was important during the testing phase, but it is even more necessary throughout the actual campaign. Monitoring allows for early detection of caller burnout—the inability of callers, through frustration and boredom, to continue making solicitation calls productively. A caller may not be aware that he or she is becoming less enthusiastic and less productive. But in monitoring calls (either with a listening device or by being present in the room), you may detect tell-tale signs: a weariness in the voice, or a monotonous delivery. If these signs are caught soon enough, you can remedy the situation. Give your caller a ten- or fifteen-minute break, perhaps change his or her seating arrangement, or arrange for a day or two off (another reason why your schedule should allow flexibility). After a rest, your caller might be able to rekindle his or her enthusiasm.

The repetitive process of calling can lead to bad speech habits. One caller may speak too quickly, another too slowly, another too softly, another may swallow words. Monitoring can give you the ability to help these callers.

Someone from your organization should be in the calling room at regular intervals; and the callers should become used to having you there. The practice of chatting with fellow callers should be discouraged because it will seriously cut into the volume of calls and distract the other callers.

INSTILLING AND MAINTAINING A SENSE OF MOMENTUM

Nothing is more important in telemarketing than conveying the urgency of your cause to the audience. This, to a large extent, depends on the enthusiasm of your callers. The callers will look to the supervisor as a model of behavior; it's a good idea for the leader of your group to take his or her turn on the telephone for an hour or two each week. This may help to identify callers' problems and will also put the group leader in direct contact with the audience. This is an invaluable help when it comes to revising your script.

SENDING OUT CONFIRMATION FORMS AND RETURN ENVELOPES

After the callers have completed their calls for the day, the staff will send out pledge forms and return envelopes to prospects who have committed to a specified amount and also to those who have indicated a willingness to give. The confirmation of pledge/commitment form is part of the telemarketing form, discussed earlier in Chapter 4. On it, your caller has filled in the amount, if known, and has added a handwritten thank you. The return envelope is a #9 or other size envelope which can accept standard-sized checks *with business reply postage paid*. If possible, confirmation forms should be sent out the day the pledge was made. It is estimated that every day you delay getting the pledge reminder to the donor/member/subscriber, 10 percent of the return is lost.

Other telemarketing forms should be sorted as follows: (1) those marked "no answer" should be kept in your active files; (2) those marked "already gave/joined/subscribed" and "unable to give this year" should be kept in a file for your next campaign; (3) those marked "wrong number" or "form incomplete—special problems" (which might indicate an unlisted number) should be put aside for special attention; and (4) those marked "no—unwilling to give" should be removed from your lists.

TABULATING RETURNS

Before long, checks will begin to arrive, and the received amounts must be recorded. In a large campaign, returns may be sent directly to a fulfillment house, but you will still need to know the actual dollars received (to compare those figures with your projected figures, and to calculate the cost per dollar raised of running your campaign).

FOLLOWING UP: THE KEY TO SUCCESS

An important key to a successful telemarketing campaign is follow-up. Your efforts on the campaign will continue long after the last phone call has been made. Follow-up reminders must be sent at one-month intervals for outstanding commitments. (As you may recall, such reminders are included in the six-part telemarketing form.) Usually, two reminders are sufficient, but if a large percentage is still outstanding after these reminders, a few callers or members from your organization may be recruited to do a telephone follow-up. It has been estimated that *the total amount received from the second and third reminders can equal the amount received from the first*. Neglecting the follow-up mailings can make the difference between a successful and an unsuccessful campaign.

CHAPTER THIRTEEN

STEP **11 Report
the Results**

Nothing is more important to running a telemarketing campaign effectively than a daily tabulation of results. Thuoo rouultu unublu your urganization to: (1) monitor the campaign on a daily basis; (2) monitor the callers; (3) evaluate script effectiveness; and (4) make practical determinations, such as the best times for calling, the best days, etc. In addition, a daily record helps to determine which segments of the audience are the most responsive, and which the least. It can help to pinpoint trouble spots and, most importantly, if the campaign is succeeding, your records provide concrete information with which to reassure top management.

After each solicitation, callers should mark the telemarketing form as follows: pledge amount (if known), maybe — send form, unwilling to give, unable to give, no answer, moved, wrong number, already joined/gave/subscribed, etc. The forms should be sorted by type of response and returned to you at the end of the day. This information provides the basis for your daily reports.

THE DAILY REPORT

The supervisor's report should take into account all of the evaluation and control criteria — that is, every factor that will help to determine the success of the campaign. Activity for each calling session should be summarized. For example, the following information should be tallied for each caller:

1. Total hours worked
2. Number of commitments — specified amount
3. Number of commitments — unspecified amount
4. Number of yes or undecided commitments per hour
5. Number of unwilling to pledge
6. Number of unable to pledge
7. Number of those who already pledged
8. Total contacts
9. Total calls attempted — no contact (moved, wrong number, etc.)

In tabulating caller information, determine:

1. Total caller hours
2. Total dollars raised in each category (with "maybes" calculated at the lowest level of giving)
3. Number of positive responses per hour
4. Number of dollars per hour
5. Percentage of positive responses from prospects contacted for each category of commitment showing both the number of commitments and total dollars

The daily report might be set up as follows: day, date and week at the top; caller names along the side; evaluation criteria, described above, at the top. An example of a daily report is shown in Figure 9.

FIGURE 9 SAMPLE DAILY PRODUCTIVITY REPORT

Sample Daily Productivity Report

	1	2	3	4	5
1	CALLER	# HRS CALLING	# HRS OTHER	TOTAL HRS	NUMBER PLEDGING A SPECIFIC $ AMT
2	L. Bunkers	7	1	8	6
3	T. Calnan	3.5	0.5	4	3
4	A. Carlson	3.5	0.5	4	13
5	K. Erickson	7			
6	J. Herzog	5			
7	T. Johnson	3.5			
8	P. Korngold	7			
9	R. Mathison	7			

	6	7	8	9
1	% TOTAL "YES/MAYBE"	VALUE OF SPECIFIED $$	% TOTAL $$ EXPECTED	AVG SPECIFIED $ AMT
2	17.14%	$80.00	9.94%	$13.33
3	17.65%	$95.00	21.35%	$31.67
4	72.22%	$200.00	63.49%	$15.38
		$165.00	23.08%	$15.00
		$130.00	17.22%	$21.67
		$115.00	26.14%	$16.43
		$185.00	11.31%	$30.83
		$75.00	13.64%	$9.38
		0.00%		$0.00
		22.88%		$12.27
		1.79%		$10.00

	10	11	12	13	14
1	# USING CREDIT CARD	% TOTAL $$ EXPECTED	VALUE OF CHARGED $$	% TOTAL $$ EXPECTED	AVG CHARGE AMT
2	0	0.00%	$0.00	0.00%	#DIV/0!
3	0	0.00%	$0.00	0.00%	#DIV/0!
4	0	0.00%	$0.00	0.00%	#DIV/0!
5	0				
6	0				
7	0				
8	0				
9	0				
10	1				
11	0				
12	0				
13					
14					

	15	16	17
1	# CONSIDERING A SPECIFIED AMT	% OF ALL "YES/MAYBE"	PROJECTED $$ CONSIDERING A SPECIFIC AMT
2	0	0.00%	$0.00
3	0	0.00%	$0.00
4	1	5.56%	$15.00
5	0		
6	0		
7	0		
8	0		
9	0		

	18	19	20
1	% OF ALL $$ COMMITTED	AVG. AMT. BEING CONSIDERED	# CONSIDERING AN UNSPECIFIED AMT
2	0.00%	#DIV/0!	29
3	0.00%	#DIV/0!	14
4	4.76%	$15.00	4
		#DIV/0!	22
		#DIV/0!	25
		#DIV/0!	13
		#DIV/0!	58
		#DIV/0!	19

	21	22	23	24	25
1	% ALL "YES/MAYBE"	PROJECTED UNSPECIFIED $$	% TOTAL $$ EXPECTED	AVG GIFT UNSPECIFIED	# UNWILLING
2	82.86%	$725.00	90.06%	$25.00	20
3	82.35%	$350.00	78.65%	$25.00	10
4	22.22%	$100.00	31.75%	$25.00	10
5	66.67%				
6	80.65%				
7	65.00%				
8	90.63%				
9	70.37%				
10	40.00%				
11	60.00%				
12	95.65%				
13					
14					

	26	27	28	29	30	31
1	# UNABLE	# ALREADY GAVE	WRONG #	#OTHER	# ATTEMPTED BUT NOT CONTACTED	CALL DAYS/OFFICE
2	53	0	18	15	70	0
3	26	2	3	3	32	1
4	24	0	7	1	48	0
5	42	0	13			
6	17	0	5			
7	13	0	13			
8	17	2	14			
9	36	0	16			

	32	33	34	35
1	SPECIAL HANDLING	TOTAL # ATTEMPTED	# CONTACTED/COMPLETED	% CONTACTED OF ATTEMPTED
2	1	212	142	66.98%
3	0	94	62	65.96%
4	0	108	60	55.56%
		231	132	57.14%
		180	75	41.67%
		113	61	53.98%
		274	172	62.77%
		242	130	53.72%
				50.79%
				63.44%
				63.11%

	36	37	38	39	40
1	TOTAL # YES/MAYBE	% CONTACTED SAYING "YES/MAYBE"	TOTAL # NO	% NO	TOTAL $$ EXPECTED
2	35	24.65%	73	51.41%	$805.00
3	17	27.42%	38	61.29%	$445.00
4	18	30.00%	34	56.67%	$315.00
5	33				
6	31				
7	20				
8	64				
9	27				
10	20				
11	30				
12	23				
13					
14					
15					
16					
17	318				
18					
19					
20					
21					
22					
23					
24					
25					
26					
27					
28					

	41	42	43	44
1	OVERALL AVG GIFT EXPECTED	WAGES/CALLER	COST/$ PER HR CALLING	OVERALL COST PER $ EXPECTED
2	$23.00	$48.00	$0.05	$0.06
3	$26.18	$24.00	$0.05	$0.05
4	$17.50	$24.00	$0.07	$0.08
5	$21.67			
6	$24.35			
7	$22.00			
8	$25.55			
9	$20.37			
10	$11.25			
11	$19.67			
12	$24.35			
13				
14				
15				
16				
17	$22.12			

	45	46	47	48	49	50	51	52
1	DIALINGS/HR	#YES/HR						
2	30.29	5.00						
3	26.86	4.86						
4	30.86	5.14						
5	33.00	4.71						
6	36.00	6.20						
7	32.29	5.71						
8	39.14	9.14						
9	34.57	3.86						
10	27.20	2.86						
11	32.43	4.29						
12	34.86	6.57						
13								
14								
15								
16								
17	32.69	5.21						
18								
19								
20								
21								
22								
23								
24								
25								
26								
27								
28								

These reports will reflect the performances of the callers. By comparing individual performances for several consecutive days, you will be able to determine which callers need help and which (if any) should be replaced.

The reports will also tell you when you generally have had a bad day. If everyone's results are off, something must be wrong. Perhaps the script needs to be changed, or the prospect list is inadequate, or your calling hours are miscalculated. Whatever the problems, these daily reports will hold the key to the first steps in solving them.

THE WEEKLY REPORT

This report is based on the combined results of your daily reports. At the top, indicate WEEK OF and fill in the dates. Along the side, list each day, Thursday through Sunday, or whatever the calling schedule is. At the top, list the evaluation criteria, such as:

1. Number of callers

2. Number of specified commitments

3. Number of unspecified commitments

4. Total pledges

5. Number of refusals

6. Total contacts

7. Percentage of pledge rate

8. Percentage of specified pledges

9. Average amount of specified pledges

Along the bottom, total all of the above. The projected dollar goal might be shown here to help determine progress. Figure 10 illustrates a sample weekly report.

THE FINAL REPORT

After the campaign is over, you should prepare a final report, based upon the cumulative results of the weekly reports. Remember your campaign doesn't end with the last phone call. It ends when the last dollar has been collected: you will be sending follow-up

FIGURE 10 SAMPLE WEEKLY REPORT

Weekly Report of Daily Results

	1	2	3	4	5
1	DATE OF CALLING	# HRS CALLING	# HRS OTHER	TOTAL HRS	# PLEDGING A SPECIFIC $ AMT.
2	Nov. 17	48.25	12.00	60.25	60
3	Nov. 18	55.50	33.00	88.50	62
4	Nov. 19	66.50	14.00	80.50	76
5	Nov. 20	52.50			
6	Nov. 21	61.00			
7	CUMULATIVE TOTALS:	283.75			

	6	7	8	9
1	% TOTAL "YES/MAYBE"	VALUE OF SPECIFIED $$	% TOTAL $$ EXPECTED	AVG SPECIFIED $ AMT
2	30.77%	$1,383.00	27.51%	$23.05
3	26.05%	$1,217.00	19.73%	$19.63
4	27.05%	$1,195.00	18.95%	$15.72
5		$813.00	12.46%	$15.34
6		$1,190.00	16.92%	$14.34
7		$3,795.00	12.22%	$11.36

	10	11	12	13	14
1	# USING CREDIT CARD	% TOTAL $$ EXPECTED	VALUE OF CHARGED $$	% TOTAL $$ EXPECTED	AVG CHARGE AMT
2	0	0.00%	$0.00	0.00%	#DIV/0!
3	1	0.42%	$50.00	0.81%	$50.00
4	0	0.00%	$0.00	0.00%	#DIV/0!
5	0				
6	1				
7	2				

	15	16	17
1	# CONSIDERING A SPECIFIED AMT	% OF ALL "YES/MAYBE"	PROJECTED $$ CONSIDERING A SPECIFIC AMT
2	27	13.85%	$945.00
3	28	11.76%	$1,225.00
4	1	0.36%	$10.00
5	6	2.	
6	2	0.	
7	64	4.	

	18	19	20
1	% OF ALL $$ COMMITTED	AVG. AMT. BEING CONSIDERED	# CONSIDERING AN UNSPECIFIED AMT
2	18.79%	$35.00	108
3	19.86%	$43.75	147
4	0.16%	$10.00	204
		$30.83	221
		$10.00	232
		$34.06	912

	21	22	23	24	25
1	% ALL "YES/MAYBE"	PROJECTED UNSPECIFIED $$	% TOTAL $$ EXPECTED	AVG GIFT UNSPECIFIED	# UNWILLING
2	55.38%	$2,700.00	53.70%	$25.00	285
3	61.76%	$3,675.00	59.59%	$25.00	180
4	72.60%	$5,100.00	80.89%	$25.00	236
5	78.93%				
6	72.96%				
7	69.51%				

	26	27	28	29	30	31
1	# UNABLE	# ALREADY GAVE	WRONG #	#OTHER	# ATTEMPTED BUT NOT CONTACTED	CALL DAYS/OFFICE
2	108	2	79	49	739	8
3	163	0	63	41	919	21
4	224	1	105	40	682	9
5	144	1	66			
6	248	5	111			
7	887	9	424			

	32	33	34	35
1	SPECIAL HANDLING TOTAL	# ATTEMPTED	# CONTACTED/COMPLETED	% CONTACTED OF ATTEMPTED
2	4	1,469	730	49.69%
3	10	1,635	716	43.79%
4	13	1,591	909	57.13%
		1,508 =	791	52.45%
		1,994	1,152	57.77%
		4,695	4,298	91.54%

	36	37	38	39	40
1	TOTAL # YES/MAYBE	% CONTACTED SAYING "YES/MAYBE"	TOTAL # NO	% NO	TOTAL $$ EXPECTED
2	195	26.71%	395	54.11%	$5,028.00
3	238	33.24%	343	47.91%	$6,167.00
4	281	30.91%	461	50.72%	$6,305.00
5	280				
6	318				
7	1,312				

	41	42	43	44
1	OVERALL AVG GIFT EXPECTED	WAGES/CALLER	COST/$ PER HR CALLING	OVERALL COST PER $ EXPECTED
2	$25.78	$361.50	$0.06	$0.07
3	$25.91	$531.00	$0.05	$0.09
4	$22.44	$546.00	$0.06	$0.09
5	$23.30			
6	$22.12			
7	$23.67			

	45	46	47	48	49	50	51	52
1	DIALINGS/HR	#YES/HR						
2	30.45	4.04						
3	29.46	4.29						
4	23.92	4.23						
5	28.72	5.33						
6	32.69	5.21						
7	16.55	4.62						

reminders on a monthly basis for at least two months, and possibly more. Once you have collected every dollar you can expect to collect, you are ready to move on to the last step of your telemarketing campaign: evaluation of the program.

CHAPTER FOURTEEN

STEP 12 Evaluate the Program

While the telemarketing program is still fresh in your mind, review and document its results. Overall contact results from several telemarketing campaigns are shown in Figure 11. The final report will be useful in planning future campaigns. Successes and failures should be easy to see if the records are in good order. If you have kept careful track of the control elements—the script, the callers, and the prospect list—evaulation will be easier.

If there were shortcomings in the campaign, you should be able to pinpoint the reasons why. Putting together all the elements that went into each day's results should give you a clear, daily picture of your campaign. You might find that you did poorly one day because you were working from a bad list. Or your script was off. Or your callers were insufficiently trained, or several of them were suffering

FIGURE **11** AUDIENCE CONTACT ANALYSIS FROM THREE RECENT TELEMARKETING CAMPAIGNS

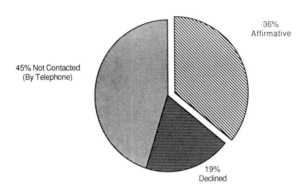

36%
Affirmative

45% Not Contacted
(By Telephone)

19%
Declined

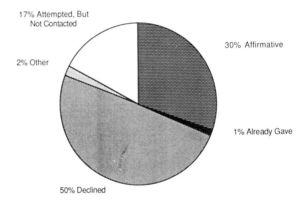

17% Attempted, But
Not Contacted

2% Other

30% Affirmative

1% Already Gave

50% Declined

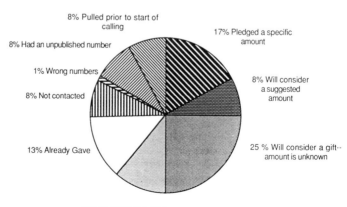

8% Pulled prior to start of
calling

8% Had an unpublished number

1% Wrong numbers

8% Not contacted

13% Already Gave

11% Negative responses

17% Pledged a specific
amount

8% Will consider
a suggested
amount

25 % Will consider a gift--
amount is unknown

from caller burnout. Whatever the case, you should be able to spot your mistakes and learn from them.

Once your organization has conducted a telemarketing campaign, the second and third campaigns will run more smoothly. You have gained experience in training callers, you have evolved a working script, and your lists now contain only prospects who have expressed interest in your organization. You will continue to refine your techniques, and those refinements will pay off in results.

Telemarketing, unfortunately, is not for everyone. If the results were disappointing, it may be because your audience doesn't know enough about your cause to want to be a part of it. Telemarketing, generally speaking, is not as cost-effective a method as direct mail for conveying detailed and complicated information to the general public. A phone call can answer questions and overcome objections, but it is not the best way to do a complicated selling job.

On the other hand, if the results were good, you obviously have an audience that is willing to listen to your message and respond. If so, you can continue to benefit from the unique and powerful advantage of telemarketing — the ability to communicate directly with your audience. Telemarketing is used to raise hundreds of thousands of dollars for groups around the country, and to bring in thousands of new donors, members, and subscribers each year. Properly applied, using the techniques described in this book, it can do the same for you.

Related Reading from ACA Books

Americans and the Arts, conducted by National Research Center of the Arts, and affiliate of Louis Harris and Associates (1984). A survey of public opinion which examines Americans' attitudes toward the arts and charts trends in their participation in and attendance at arts activities. 122 pages. Price: $5.00.

The Buck Starts Here: Enterprise in the Arts edited by Robert Karl Manoff. Transcript from conference on the legal aspects and implications of profit making ventures in the nonprofit sector. Published by Volunteer Lawyers for the Arts (1984). ISBN 0-917103-00-9 165 pages. Price: $9.95.

Directory of Matching Gift Programs. A directory of corporations nationwide which have matching gift programs. Published by Business Committe for the Arts, Inc. (1984). 45 pages. Price: $5.00.

Effective Corporate Fundraising by W. Grant Brownrigg. Maps out a clear, concise comprehensive strategy for conducting a systematic and effective corporate fundraising campaign. Published by American Council for the Arts (1982). ISBN 0-915400-37-5 162 pages Price: $12.95.

Enterprise in the Nonprofit Sector by James C. Crimmins and Mary Neil. A resource guide which explores the issues, risks, and benefits involved as nonprofits tap previously ignored money sources through innovative entrepreneurial ventures. Published by Partners for Livable Places (1983). ISBN 0-941182-03-7 141 pages. Price: $7.00.

Financial Management Stategies for Arts Organizations by Robert Gallo and Frederick Turk. Outlines financial concepts and processes and how they can be used to construct sophisticated strategies for handling resources—people, money, and facilities—which can result in more effective and successful programs. Published by American Council for the Arts (1984). ISBN 0-915400-40-5 200 pages. Price: $17.95.

Guide to Corporate Giving edited by Robert A. Porter. A thorough and useful directory which contains information on the giving policies of over 700 major corporations. Published by American Council for the Arts (1983). ISBN 0-915400-39-1 592 pages. Price: $30.00.

Help! A Guide to Seeking, Selecting and Surviving an Arts Consultant by Joseph Golden. A timely guide to identifying and selecting the right consultant for an arts organization. Published by Cultural Resources Council (1983). 56 pages. Price: $6.50.

Helping People Volunteer by Judy Rauner. Practical information on how to create and implement volunteer programs within a community and/or organization. Published by Marlborough Publications (1980). ISBN 0-9604594-0-5 82 pages. Price: $9.95.

Live the Good Life! Creating a Human Community through the Arts by Wolf Von Eckardt. An expansive appeal to anyone interested in urban revitalization, historic preservation, city planning or any other activity for enhancing the quality of life in American cities through the arts and the necessity of government involvement in this undertaking. Published by American Council for the Arts (1982). ISBN 0-915400-24-3 129 pages. Price: $7.50

Market the Arts edited by Joseph Melillo. This information packed marketing handbook anthology aids the novice and professional by detailing time-tested marketing techniques so that any arts organization can compete more effectively in a crowded arts marketplace. Published by FEDAPT (1983). ISBN 0-910755-03-5 40 pages. Price: $19.95.

The Media Resource Guide. A concise and straightforward introduction to good newsmedia relations. Published by Foundation for American Communications (1983). ISBN 0-910755-03-5 40 pages. Price: $5.00.

The Nonprofit Organization by Thomas Wolf. Provides essential information on planning, creating and sustaining a nonprofit organization. Published by Prentice-Hall, Inc. (1984). ISBN 0-13-623315-5 184 pages. Price: $8.95.

Nonprofit Piggy Goes to Market by Robin Simons, Lisa Farber Miller, and Peter Lengsfelder. A blueprint for success in the nonprofit marketplace, this step-by-step guide details enterprising ideas that can mean more money for any organization. Published by Children's Museum of Denver (1984). 31 pages. Price: $7.50.

No Quick Fix (Planning) edited by Frederic B. Vogel. This "how-to" book underscores the necessity of careful and thoughtful management of personnel, finances, and physical resources. Published by FEDAPT (1985). ISBN 0-960294-5-2 96 pages. Price: $9.95.

Subscribe Now! by Danny Newman. A step-by-step handbook for subscription promotion and audience development. Published by Theatre Communications Group (1977). ISBN 0-930452-01-1 276 pages. Price: $10.95.

United Arts Fundraising Campaign Analysis edited by Robert A. Porter. A detailed study of more than 55 federated drives nationwide which raise money for the arts. Published by American Council for the Arts (1985). ISBN 0-915400-5-0 80 pages. Price: $20.00.

United Arts Fundraising Policybook. Provides nuts and bolts details on how to set up a united arts fund or improve an existing one by listing the bylaws, policies, and procedures of twelve large and small united arts funds nationwide. 270 pages. Price: $125.00.

For more information on these books, write for a free publications catalog to: ACA Books, Dept. MD 134. 570 Seventh Avenue, New York, NY 10018.

ABOUT THE AMERICAN COUNCIL FOR THE ARTS

The American Council for the Arts (ACA) addresses significant issues in the arts by promoting communications, management improvement, and problem-solving among those who shape and implement arts policy. ACA currently accomplishes this by:

- fostering communication and cooperation among arts groups and leaders in the public and private sectors;
- promoting advocacy on behalf of *all* the arts;
- sponsoring research, analysis, studies;
- publishing books, manuals, *Vantage Point*, and *ACA Update* for leaders and managers in the arts;
- providing information and clearinghouse services;
- providing technical assistance to arts managers and administrators.

BOARD OF DIRECTORS

Chairman of the Board
Donald G. Conrad

President
Milton Rhodes

Vice Chairmen
Edward M. Block
Eugene C. Dorsey
Stephen Stamas

Secretary
John Kilpatrick

Treasurer
Linda Hoeschler

Other Members
Jane Alexander
Ben Barkin
Anne Bartley
Theodore Bikel

John Brademas
Mrs. George P. Caulkins, Jr.
Marshall Cogan
Colleen Dewhurst
Barbaralee Diamonstein-
 Spielvogel
Peter Duchin
Mrs. Robert Fowler
Jack Golodner
Toni Goodale
Donald R. Greene
Eldrige C. Hanes
David H. Harris
Louis Harris
Richard Hunt
Susan Kelly
Mrs. Fred Lazarus III
Robert Leys
Victor Macdonald
Lewis Manilow
James M. McClymond

Velma V. Morrison
Michael Newton
Alwin Nikolais
Mrs. Charles D. Peebler
Murray Charles Pfister
Mrs. Richard S.
 Reynolds III
David Rockefeller, Jr.
Henry C. Rogers
Rodney Rood
Terry T. Saario
Daniel I. Sargent
Frank Saunders
Edward Saxe
Sam F. Segnar
Mary Shands
John Straus
Roselyne C. Swig
Esther Wachtell
Mrs. Gerald Westby
Mrs. Gayle Wilson

MAJOR CONTRIBUTORS

At press time, special thanks are extended to the following
for their contributions in support of ACA's operations, programs,
and special projects.

BENEFACTORS ($40,000 and up)

American Telephone & Telegraph Company • CBS Inc.
Marshall S. Cogan • Digital Equipment Corporation • Exxon Corporation
Gannett Foundation •InterNorth, Inc. • Knoll International

SUSTAINERS ($20,000 to $39,999)

Aetna Life & Casualty Foundation • Atlantic Richfield Company
Edward M. Block • Louis Harris & Associates
Philip Morris Incorporated
Rockefeller Foundation • San Francisco Foundation

PATRONS ($10,000 to $19,999)

NW Ayer Inc. • Bay Foundation • Dayton Hudson Corporation
Equitable Life Assurance Society • Mrs. Ruth Lilly
National Endowment for the Arts
Murray Charles Pfister • Progressive Corporation
Mr. and Mrs. David Rockefeller, Jr. • Reverend and Mrs. Alfred Shands, III
Mr. and Mrs. Richard L. Swig

DONORS ($5,000 to $9,999)

The Allstate Foundation • American Stock Exchange
The Arts and Entertainment Network
BATUS Inc. • Bell Atlantic • The Mary Duke Biddle Foundation
Chesebrough-Pond's Inc. • The Chevron Fund • The Coca-Cola Foundation
Donald G. Conrad • Barbaralee Diamonstein-Spielvogel • Eastman Kodak
Ford Motor Company Fund • General Electric Foundation
Gund Foundation, Inc. • IBM Corporation • ITT
Susan Kelly • John Kilpatrick, Jr. • Loral Corporation
Lewis Manilow • Mobil Foundation, Inc.
New York State Council on the Arts • Peat, Marwick, Mitchell & Co.
PepsiCo Foundation • Phillips Petroleum Foundation
Prudential Insurance Company Foundation • R.J. Reynolds
Henry C. Rogers • RCA Corporation • Rockefeller Group
Shell Companies Foundation • Standard Oil Company (Ohio)
Union Pacific Foundation
Warner Communications Inc. • Mrs. Gerald H. Westby
Whirlpool Corporation • Xerox Corporation

CONTRIBUTORS ($2,000 to $4,999)

Alcoa Foundation • Allied Corporation • Bankers Trust Company
Brakeley, John Price Jones Inc. • Bristol-Myers Fund • Dart & Kraft, Inc.
Drexel Burnham • Emerson Electric Company
Federated Department Stores, Inc. • Mr. & Mrs. Robert Fowler
Hartmarx Corporation • Mr. and Mrs. John G. Hoeschler
Knight Foundation • Lazard Freres & Company
New York Life Foundation • New York Times Company Foundation
NL Industries Foundation, Inc. • Mrs. Charles Peebler
J. C. Penney Company, Inc. • Procter & Gamble Fund
Mrs. Pamela Coe Reynolds • Raytheon Company
Daniel I. Sargent • Sears, Roebuck & Company • U.S. Steel Foundation
John Strauss • Westinghouse Electric Fund

FRIENDS ($1,000 to $1,999)

American Broadcasting Companies, Inc.
American Can Company Foundation • Anne Bartley • Bell South
Ben Barkin • Bechtel Foundation • Binney & Smith
Bozell & Jacobs, Inc. • Carter Hawley Hale Stores, Inc.
Mrs. George P. Caulkins, Jr. • CIGNA Corporation
Conoco, Inc. • Cooper Industries • Mr. and Mrs. Earle M. Craig, Jr.
CSX Corporation • Mrs. Catherine G. Curran • Ethyl Corporation
Arthur Gelber • General Dynamics Corporation • Toni K. Goodale
Gulf + Western Foundation • Hanes Companies, Inc.
H. J. Heinz Company Foundation • Mr. & Mrs. John J. Heinz
Hercules, Inc. • Knight-Ridder Newspapers, Inc. • Stephen Kovacs
Krissel Foundation • Arthur Levitt, Jr.
Robert Leys • Manufacturers Hanover Trust
James M. McClymond • Mr. and Mrs. Robert Merrill
Metropolitan Life Foundation • Mrs. Velma V. Morrison
National Computer Systems • Pfizer Foundation, Inc.
Readers Digest Corporation • Mrs. Samuel P. Reed • Milton Rhodes
Felix Rohatyn • Rubbermaid Incorporated • Salomon Brothers Inc.
Frank A. Saunders • Scurlock Oil Company • Sam F. Segnar
Textron Charitable Trust • Times-Mirror Company • Touche Ross & Co.
Donald J. Trump • Esther Wachtell
Lila Acheson Wallace Fund • Lawrence A. Wein

ABOUT THE AUTHORS

MICHAEL E. BLIMES is chairman of the MIDAS Group, Inc., a Minneapolis-based fundraising management, membership marketing, and information systems consulting firm. For nearly 15 years, he has been involved in fundraising, membership, and subscription marketing programs and campaigns which have incorporated direct-marketing strategies for the effective use of direct mail and telemarketing. Prior to forming the MIDAS Group in 1983, he served as senior consultant with C.W. Shaver & Company, Inc., a New York City-based consulting firm known for its management and marketing consulting, and fundraising counsel in the arts. Mr. Blimes is an experienced manager and director of fundraising programs in higher education, and currently serves as executive director of the Colorado State University Foundation. He has previously held positions at Ohio State University, Albion College, and American Graduate School. He is a 1971 graduate in journalism from Ohio State University, and has complemented his practical experience with graduate study in public relations and international marketing.

RON SPROAT is a free-lance writer who lives and works in New York City. More than a dozen of his plays have been produced for stage and for television. He is a former head writer for the classic television serial "Dark Shadows" and has written for a number of other television series. His articles have been published in a variety of magazines, including *New York* and *Paris Match*. M Drama School.

89